Isla

By Riva Fidel Robinson, M.D.

To my dearest niece adela Riva tu tio

Printed in the United States of America

First Printing: April 2010

ISBN 978-0-557-41994-4

Table of Contents Preface

Acknowledgements

Acknowledgements

I want to show my utmost appreciation to the following people for contributing to make this book possible.

First, I want to thank my wife, Vivien Townsend Robinson, for her helping to organize the material and for putting the text into modern English.

Second, I want to thank my granddaughter, Abbe Robinson, for putting the material on the computer.

Third, I want to thank my granddaughter, Erika Robinson and my grandson, Ryan Robinson for the excellent format and for arranging the pictures.

Fourth, I want to thank Mrs. Magda Archbold for letting me use a few of her island pictures in this book.

Fifth, I would like to express my gratitude to Gilberto Marroquin for the beautiful painting of the Klondike, Haines Cay, and Coco Plum Point in San Andres that adorns the cover of this book.

Finally, I would like to thank my dear friend, Joseph Gress, for editing, correcting and getting the book into printed form.

Preface

The islands of San Andres and Providencia are two specs on the map of the Caribbean Sea. They are in the western part of the Caribbean Sea one hundred miles from the main land of Central America. The natives of these islands act as if the universe rotates around them. I am a native of these islands and in some respects I agree with my countrymen even though I have traveled extensively. The history of these islands is fascinating and the stories about them are incredible. In this little book I have reproduced some of the stories as I either experienced them or as they were told to me. The history, as I have tried to relate accurately, come from two sources: first the oral history, passed down from one generation to the next. It is interesting and colorful. Some of this history is correct, and some false. The history that is the result of research is for the most part correct but there are also errors for the following reasons: first, some of the historians copy from the history and research of previous ones. Second, original sources are limited. Third, some historians have spent limited time on the islands and their conclusions are not always correct. Fourth, at times there is a language barrier. Fifth, at times the islanders themselves will deliberately mislead the historian. There are times when the research is excellent and others when it is not so good. Sometimes the history that is researched from previous sources is correct and occasionally the oral history is better. In this book I have tried to be as historically correct as possible and where the facts are controversial I have included both sides of the question. However, this is not primarily a history book, but just stories, but each anecdote is based on historical fact. In the last chapter the stories are of my immediate family. I did spend my early life, up to my mid-teens, on the islands and since then I have never been out of touch with our culture. Finally, I hope you enjoy these stories like I do in telling them. I like history and I love stories. This is not a religious book but religion is an integral part of our island culture and some of the stories do have a religious flavor. I make no apologies for the religious tone in any of these anecdotes. Religion is an integral part of my own life. Finally, this book is primarily dedicated to my immediate family, to my lovely wife Vivian Townsend Robinson, my brothers and sisters, my children, and the memory of Walter and Crisilda Robinson, my parents. I hope you, reader, enjoy Island Anecdotes as I enjoyed writing them.

Chapter 1—History 1500 to 1800

Discovery

I, Riva Robinson, was 13 years old when I sat in the bow of our 12' canoe. I was being drenched with sea spray with the spray in the air all around me. I was helping my father paddle our boat towards home. As we turned McKellar Point at the end of the Island, my Dad said, "Put up the sail." I tried unsuccessfully to do so, but the sail fell into the sea, and the boat filled with water. On the second try, the sail was put in place, and we sailed home at a brisk pace.

Dad and I had left home on Providencia around 5 a.m. The full moon illuminated the water. The coconut palms added to the magic of the moment. Then there was no sign of bad weather, as we traveled over a calm sea to the plantation on Santa Catalina. Sufficient mangos and coconuts were harvested, and when we started back the boat was quite loaded with fruits. As we got outside of the cove, we were hit with the full force of the storm.

Meanwhile, mother and the remainder of the children were weeping because they were sure that father and I had perished in the open ocean, taking the brunt of the storm. But when the boat came to the landing, tears, moans and groans turned to shouts of joy!

This is part of everyday life on the Island of Providencia—moments of tropical paradise bliss changed to moments of despair!

But let's start where it all began. The Islands of San Andres, Providencia, and Santa Catalina with their surrounding cays, are located approximately 80 miles off the coast of what is now Nicaragua. The two main islands are separated by 50 miles of ocean. Providencia is located 50 miles north of San Andres.

Map showing Providencia and San Andres relative to Nicaragua, Panama and Colombia

Satellite photo of San Andres

Sprat Bight Beach, San Andres

San Andres is a coral island, being flat with a promontory in the middle, running north and south with the highest point being 240.' From the air it appears as a big coconut plantation. This is changing, however, where hotels are mushrooming to replace the coconut palms. There is a reef that partially surrounds the Island of San Andres which varies from 2 to 3 1/2 miles out from the Island. It starts at the North end of the Island where there is a cay called "Johnny Cay," and extends towards the South, but not reaching the South end of the Island. There's no reef on the West side of San Andres, but ships can anchor on this leeward side of the Island. The main seaport is on the eastern side with the entrance being a break in the reef about the size of a football field. It is a beautiful island with many white, sandy beaches. It is 7 miles long by 3 miles in the widest part, and in the shape of a sea horse.

Once I was on a flight from Puerto Rico to Miami. I was sitting by the window, in the seat next to me was a German lady and in the seat next to her sat a lady from Canada. These two women were having a lively conversation about their travels. By the way they were talking I could tell both had traveled extensively. They were both talking about their many travels. The Canadian lady asked the lady from Germany, "In your many travels where in your opinion is the most beautiful place you have been?" Without hesitating the German lady responded, "Of all the places where I have been, the most beautiful is a little island in the Western Caribbean that belongs to Colombia named San Andres." I had been dozing but when that German lady said that I suddenly was wide awake. I interrupted her, "What did you say lady?" After I told her that I was a native of San Andres she assured me that San Andres was the most beautiful place that she had seen. Of course she had not seen Providencia.

The Island of Providencia, on the other hand, is of volcanic origin with most of the surface covered with hills and some valleys in between. Providencia is oval shaped of approximately 4 miles long by 4 miles wide. The highest point is High Peak at 1167' above sea level with its sister peak, known as Peggy Shine Head, only a few feet lower. On a clear day these peaks can be seen from San Andres. Seen from High Peak, the Island looks like a giant turtle. Providencia is almost surrounded by a mostly coral reef, being the second largest barrier reef in the New World with the first being located in Belize.

The Providencia reef ranges from 9 1/2 miles to the North, and there it ends in a small rocky cay, leaving the Island of

Santa Catalina's north and west coast exposed to open ocean. The reef ends around the Southwest side of the Island, coming as close as 2 miles to the Island at Rocky Point.

Providencia is considered to be one of the most beautiful islands of the world, as stated by historian Cabrera Ortiz.

Split Hill, Providencia

This beauty is sworn to by many people, including a close friend of our family, Devan Mullins, who is a very successful attorney. A few years ago, he took a break from his practice, bought a boat, and sailed around the world. Towards the end of his voyage, he was coming up the eastern Florida coast, and he stopped to see his friend, Dr. Rhonda Robinson Ringer. During his visit with Rhonda, she said,

"Devan, with all the places you've seen, including the South Pacific, the Caribbean, and the East Indies, where is the most beautiful place in the world?"

Devan answered, "The most beautiful place in the world is a small island in the western Caribbean."

"What's the name of the place?" Rhonda asked.

"There's no use telling you because you or anybody else would not know the place, he said.

Rhonda insisted, "Tell me the name of the place."

Finally, Devan said, "The Island of Providencia in the western Caribbean is the most beautiful spot in the world!"

and he added, "Instead of staying there the 3 days I had planned, I stayed 3 weeks! The people are most interesting."

Rhonda exclaimed, "That's where my Dad is from!"

There are rumors that these islands were discovered by Christopher Columbus in 1504 on his fourth voyage. It is stated that on going from Veragua (today's Panama) to the Island of Hispanola (today's Dominican Republic) that he saw the Island of Providencia, but the truth is that Columbus never saw either of these islands. Instead the islands were discovered by two Spaniards whose names were Alonso de Ojeda and Diego de Nicuesa.

Actually Diego de Nicuesa got separated from Ojeda. He became the real discoverer. He stayed a few days riding out a storm. This was November 25, 1510. It was Captain Olano of one of Nicuesa's ships that first saw the island. Nicuesa didn't find any permanent residents on these Islands. However, he found an abundance of wild tropical fruits and an abundance of drinking water. Providencia was uninhabited at the time, excepting for the occasional visits of Miskito Indians, seeking turtles and fish. San Andres was discovered November 30, 1510. For the next several years, the Islands were mainly visited by adventurers, pirates and contrabandists. During the 1500s very few Europeans made their permanent homes in these Islands

Before the Europeans came to America, the Miskito Indians of Central America would come especially to Providencia to hunt turtles and to fish. So the Spaniards were the real discoverers of these island jewels. They gave them the names of San Andres and Santa Catalina respectively because of the saints' names of the day on which they were found.

The following chart may help clarify the different names that have been used for these islands over the centuries:

Modern Name	San Andres	Providencia	Santa Catalina
Dutch Name	Henrietta	Saint Catherine	
English Name	Henrietta / Saint Andrews	Saint Catherine / Old Providence	
Original Spanish	San Andres	Santa Catalina	Providencia
Current Spanish	San Andres	Providencia	Santa Catalina

The Dutch gave the name of Henrietta to what is now San Andres, and the British gave the name of Saint Catherine to what is now Providencia, and Santa Catalina was named Old

Providence. Later they reversed the names of these two islands. There has always been some confusion for the Island of Providencia, which was Old Providence, but is somewhat confused with Providence, Rhode Island and New Providence of the Bahamas. Old Providence is English and Providencia has always been the name given by the Spaniards. St. Andrews, which at first was called Henrietta given that name by the Dutch for San Andres.

During the 1500s there were very few permanent residents on these islands. Even though they were claimed by Spain, Dutch and English privateers would use the islands for their base of operations.

Pedro Serrano

In the year 1517, a Spanish ship was wrecked on the reef surrounding a group of cays 80 miles north of Providencia. Everyone on board was lost with the exception of a Spanish sailor called Pedro Serrano, who being an excellent swimmer was able to swim to shore, arriving there in a state of complete exhaustion. These cays were later named Serrana, in honor of Pedro Serrano. He survived by eating raw crabs, shrimp and turtles. He would turn the turtles on their backs and kill them with the knife he had managed to salvage from the ship. He would then drink the blood, eat the meat, raw at first, and then somehow managed to start a fire. There were no springs on the cay, so Serrano would use the turtle shells for collecting rain water. It is possible that there were a few coconut palms on the cay also to supplement his miserable diet.

The Serrana Cays have been visited from prehistorical times where sea birds by the millions would come to lay their eggs. People from Providencia would go there, and fill their boats with these eggs. Doubtless, Pedro Serrano would supplement his diet with these eggs at certain times of the year. Pedro was on the cay in this pitiful condition for 3 years. Needless to say, by this time his clothes had rotted away, leaving him completely naked.

One day he was very surprised to see a man coming towards him. The man had been shipwrecked under similar circumstances. He managed to get to the beach, clinging to a wooden plank from the unfortunate ship, and was the only survivor of this shipwreck.

These two men spent the next 4 years alone on this cay. There was a short time when the 2 men quarreled, and did not talk to each other, but they soon realized that cooperation made their lives more bearable.

After 7 years of Serrano being on this isolated place, a Spanish ship saw the smoke from their camp, and a lifeboat was dispatched to investigate the situation. They picked them up, and the ship proceeded to Spain. The companion of Serrano died during the voyage. But Serrano was in good health, and toured Western Europe especially Germany and Austria under the promotion of Charles V. His body was completely covered by hair, so that he looked more like a savage animal instead of a human being. The hair of his head was very long which sometimes would get in his way. Needless to say, Serrano was splendidly remunerated for these tours, and passed the rest of his life in luxury. This story was made public by the famous Peruvian Indian author, Garsilazo de la Vega.

Colonization

As stated above, Diego de Nicuesa discovered the Island of Providencia on November 25, 1510, and the Island of San Andres five days later on November 30, 1510.

Following the custom of the Spaniards, he named those Islands in accordance with the Saint's Day on which they were discovered. The first Island was named Santa Catalina according to the Saint's Day of November 25. The small Island attached to it was named Providencia. As we know them now, the names are reversed. He named the other Island San Andres, also according to the Saint's Day on which he found it.

But the Dutch and British shortly after started to call San Andres Henrietta. By 1527 there was a world map published which included Santa Catalina, San Andres and the Serrana Bank and a smaller bank called Serranilla. It was about this time that British, Dutch, and French adventurers and privateers started to frequent the Caribbean and Central American areas, in search of seaports in order to establish themselves as trading partners with the American natives, and with other seamen like themselves, and to raid on the Spanish shipping.

The Dutchmen were experts in ship building, and they built a dry dock in Providencia Harbor where they would haul up their vessels for repairs. They soon started to build ships also with the excellent timber of cedar, mahogany and fustick. San Andres was especially famous for its cedar and Providencia for its fustick. The fustick, a very hard wood, was used for the stem and for the planks that formed the frame of the vessel. Much of the timber they exploited, and took to the dry docks in Holland. This trade continued approximately 100 years before other seamen would venture to colonize the Islands. Among the Dutchmen who made frequent visits to the Islands was Captain Abraham Bluefields. He was in charge of cutting wood for export especially on Providencia. He also was busy with pillaging the Spanish ships. He also founded the village bearing his name, Bluefields in what is now Nicaragua.

Another Dutchman, Captain John Haine established himself on the eastern side of San Andres (or Henrietta as they called it at that time) and we have his name on Haine's Cay and also Haine's Bight.

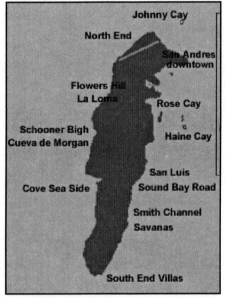

Map showing Haines Cay and other locations on San Andres

Captain Haine exploited the forest of San Andres with a group of woodsmen, then planted the deforested land with cotton, corn and other food products. Captains Bluefields and Haine revised the charts that the Spaniards had made, and began selling them especially to the Englishmen. These charts were more accurate and detailed than the former ones. Without a doubt, the Puritans at least had one of these charts.

The Puritan leaders before establishing themselves in Virginia and New England of North America, had visited the

Island of Providencia. The Puritans selected this area for the establishment of their colony after the failures of their colony in Bermuda due to unfavorable weather.

It must be kept in mind that the Spaniards had claimed these islands as part of their territory, but showed no interest in colonizing them, due to the fact there were no gold, silver or other precious metals. It was only after many attacks by the English privateers that the Spaniards began to show some interest in occupying, but not in colonizing the Islands.

In 1627, the colony of Bermuda was completely bankrupt. Their crops of tobacco had dwindled into insignificance, making them to see the need to seek a safer and more fertile place. Bermuda was ravished by tropical storms at that time. Captain Cammock was one of the principal stockholders of the Colonial Company who scouted the southwestern Caribbean, and chose the Island of Providencia as the best location to which to relocate. It was Captain Cammock who brought 30 Pilgrims to the Island of Henrietta on the Ship Earl of Warwick in 1627.

In spite of the fact that this first group went to San Andres, the company made Providencia its real location. Captain Cammock belonged to a group of persecuted people because of their fundamental religious beliefs.

In October of 1629, Captain Daniel Elfrith, Commanding Officer of the Ship Roberts, reached Providencia after stopping at San Andres, to pick up Captain Needman, whom he took to Providencia, and left Captain Axe as Commanding Officer at San Andres. On August 30 of 1630, the Spanish governor of Cartagena, being informed of English people living on San Andres which was considered a Spanish possession, dispatched Captain Gregorio Castelar to clear San Andres completely of Englishmen. Captain Axe evacuated all the cabins, and took all the people to a high part of the Island. Captain Castelar landed in the cove on the southwestern side of the Island where he found no one because they were hiding in the forest. He then returned to Cartagena, and informed his superiors that the Island was completely unoccupied.

In February of 1631, Captain Elfrith left England in command of the Sea Flower. It is interesting that a similar name was given to the Mayflower which went to Massachusetts. The Sea Flower reached Providencia with 90 Pilgrims to reinforce the colony. The Pilgrims then built 30 cabins and a brick church, and named their village New Westminster. This area is now known as Old Town. The Puritans planted tobacco against their religious scruples, and against the advice of their religious leaders. Tobacco was their chief export and money crop. They also grew cotton, indigo and corn. The investors in this venture made large investments, but their returns were exceeded by their expenses, and the company slowly started to fail.

By the end of 1631, there were 500 white men on Providencia, 40 women and 90 Black slaves. Because of the shortage of white women, some of the Englishmen established good relations with the Chief of the Miskito Indians of Central America and brought back Miskito Indian women with permission of the chief. Thus the Islanders not only traced their rich cultural lineage to their European and African roots, but also to the native Americans.

By 1640, in New Westminster, they had built 14 fortifications with 56 canons and 148 muskets. They also had 600 European men trained to use guns. On May 30, 1640, Captain Antonio Maldonado y Tejada came to Providencia with orders from the Spanish Governor of Cartagena to rid the Island of Englishmen. He came with 7 ships and 800 soldiers and 200 fighting Black slaves. Upon entering the channel of Southwest Bay, the British opened fire on his fleet. The defense was a success, and Captain Maldonado had to retreat, losing one of his ships and about 100 men. Some of the Spanish survivors managed to reach the beach, but were captured and executed by Governor Carter of New Westminster, in spite of the protests of the Puritan Pastors. The slaughter of the Spanish seamen by Governor Carter only served to increase the hatred of the Spanish towards the Englishmen. A year later, May 6, 1641, the Spanish once again attacked the Island under the command of Captain Francisco Diaz de Pimienta which left Cartagena with 11 battleships, 1400 soldiers and 600 marines. They reached Providencia on the l9th of May, and anchored on the southeastern side of the Island where there were no defenses. After scouting the hills with his men, Diaz de Pimienta decided to attack from Smooth Water Bay, and proceeded to climb over the steep hills overlooking the village of New Westminster. All the women and children were alone here because all the men were at the forts because the British thought the Spaniards would attack the forts.

On the morning of the twenty-fourth, the Spanish soldiers swarmed down the hillsides. The British Governor Fitch had left the town totally unguarded. As a result 350 people, including slaves surrendered. The rest of mostly single men and slaves, escaped in small boats, some of them reaching San

Andres and Corn Island, and some were taken by the currents to the mainland. During the attack 20 Englishmen and 5 Spaniards died. Many weapons were captured by the Spaniards. Governor Fitch informed Captain Diaz de Pimienta that the Island of San Andres was unoccupied and that all of the men had come to Providencia to help defend it. Captain Gregorio Castelar was sent to San Andres to find out the truth. Castelar confirmed that San Andres was totally unoccupied. Actually, all the inhabitants had hidden themselves in the hills, from where they could observe the movement of the enemy which could not see them. No lamps were lit at night, and they were careful to put out all fires. It is said that more than 500 colonists had escaped from Providencia.

With the expulsion of the Puritans, and the recapture of the Islands by Francisco Diaz de Pimienta, the Spaniards were in charge of the Islands for approximately the next 30 years.

Morgan's Head

Picture of the Pirate John Henry Morgan

The British Vengeance

From 1641 to 1662 the islands were governed by the Spanish. Thereafter control went back and forth between the British and the Spanish. This period was dominated by pirates, privateers, and smugglers. As stated previously, the islands were used by the pirates as a base of operations to attack the Spanish galleons and the Spanish settlements. When the pirates would land on Providencia and San Andres they would not torture or kill the inhabitants but would use the port for their operations. The people who lived on these islands, if they had any money would bury it. After the pirates left, they would retrieve the money. Very often they would forget where they buried the money and so it was lost to them, only to be found by others many years later, even hundreds of years later. So, the treasure could be buried by the pirates or by the people of the islands themselves. The treasure was usually in the form of gold coins, gold bullion, or jewels. Whenever a pirate ship was sighted the people of the islands would hurriedly bury whatever items of value they owned and flee to the hills to hide. The pirates would usually only use the ports and forts on the periphery of the islands. This was their custom, especially on San Andres. The pirates would anchor their ships in the cove but would not disturb the people hiding in the hills. Even on occasion the pirates would trade freely with the islanders. The Spanish warships tried to defend themselves against the pirates but the pirates were successful in enriching themselves with the Spanish booty. On one occasion the English pirate Mitchell was surprised by a Spanish warship while in the harbor of San Andres. Mitchell took off and timed the ocean swells perfectly to get over the reef without damage to his ship.

On another occasion five men in a small boat tried to pillage a boat from Central America. However a west wind came up and drove them into the Roncador Key where they lost their boat. These men then were in the dire circumstances that Pedro Serrano had endured decades earlier. There are no springs on Roncador and the small amount of water that they obtained was from the rain falling into the shells of the turtles that were captured. So they ate turtles and bird eggs. One by one the men died. At the end of two-and-a-half years there was only one man left alive. He was picked up by a ship and was taken to Providencia.

This was the only period in the history of the islands when Spanish was the dominant language and Catholicism the main religion.

Cave entrance on Santa Catalina

In the year 1660 the famous Dutch pirate Edward Mansfeld, who was the most outstanding privateer of that time, had as a member of his crew a 20 year old Welsh man by the name of John Henry Morgan who learned the elements of piracy from Mansfeld. At this time Morgan was subordinate to Mansfeld but in just a few years Morgan became the most outstanding pirate of all time. Morgan used Jamaica as his main headquarters but he used Providencia as his base of operations when it was advantageous. He used Providencia as his starting point to capture Panama City as he had done to capture Maracaibo and Portobelo. Morgan became fabulously rich. He buried a large part of his treasure on the island of Santa Catalina in one or more of the caves that are found there. At least one cave has its entrance under water (with which cave I am familiar) but the inside of the cave is above water so that access has to be made by a short dive. The cave has rooms going off in many directions so Morgan would place his treasure in one or more of these rooms. It is said that he would kill a slave and bury him along with the treasure so that the spirit of the slave would guard the treasure. There are stories that go along with this as the treasures seem to be haunted.

John Henry Morgan was born in Wales of the British Isles. His father was an Anglican. His mother was an Irish Catholic. She was kidnapped by Edward Mansfeld and taken to England where she married John Henry Morgan's father. The senior Morgan would ill treat his wife whenever she mentioned that she was a Catholic but she secretly taught John Henry the rosary and the Catholic prayers. John Henry's father signed him on a ship under Mansfeld when he was still a teenager. By the time John Henry was 20 years old he was the subordinate of Mansfeld. Morgan was taught the essentials of being a pirate by Mansfeld and soon became a first class buccaneer in his own right, even becoming more famous than Mansfeld. John Henry Morgan became the most famous pirate of all time.

The island of Providencia is strategically located directly in the route used by the Spanish convoys. Spain used the ports of Cartagena, Portobelo, Veracruz and Havana for all trade with the mother country so there would be several Spanish ships going in a convoy at any given time. Providencia was an ideal location for attacking these Spanish shipping convoys and was used by the pirates as their home base. Morgan made the island of Santa Catalina one of his principal bases for attacking the Spanish Main, as well as attacking Spanish shipping in general. At other times Jamaica was used as headquarters. The islands of Providencia and Santa Catalina were separated, first by Morgan and later by Aury, by a canal. Morgan had his main fort on Santa Catalina but three other forts were also placed strategically in Providencia. These forts were actually built by the Spaniards earlier. Morgan used the islands of Providencia and Santa Catalina to attack the Spaniards of Portobelo and Panama City.

On one occasion Morgan's ships attacked Santa Marta (in what is now Colombia). His subordinates inflicted one of the worst disasters on this port. After sacking the town and committing various atrocities to the people they took Bishop Lucas Fernandez Piedrahita prisoner. The bishop was a great historian and one of the most illustrious clergymen that New Granada (now Colombia) had at that time. Even though he was born in the new world he had the privilege, on one memorable occasion, to perform religious services for the monarch of Spain. When he was surprised by the pirates he was preparing to go to Panama to preside over that diocese. The pirates did a lot of damage and they violated the area that the bishop used for keeping his sacred objects. The clergyman was made a prisoner. The pirates took him to Providencia and presented him to Morgan. The surprising thing was that the pirate Morgan received the bishop in a very cordial manner, even having some of his personal objects returned to him that had been stolen by the pirates, including his signet ring. Thus it was that Providencia had in its territory the illustrious bishop whose deportment left Morgan with an indelible impression. When the buccaneers who had invaded Santa Marta came to Providencia they gave Morgan the treasure that they had obtained and told him that they had as prisoner Bishop Piedrahita. Morgan asked these men how they had captured the bishop. Those who had ill treated the bishop joked at the question and made fun of that saintly man. Morgan interrupted them with the shout, "Silence!", then he turned to his guard, stating, "Shut these men up in the most secure dungeon and please go and bring me the saintly bishop." The pirates were surprised but obeyed Morgan's orders. Morgan was a man who did not have compassion on anyone so they did not understand what was happening.

"Most reverend and illustrious bishop," said Morgan, "you see me here, ashamed and confused."

"You being ashamed and confused!" exclaimed the bishop with surprise. He had heard many times of the cruel acts of this pirate and he was only waiting for the new insult that he was to receive.

"Yes sir. I am full of shame because of the conduct of my officials and soldiers in Santa Marta regarding you because you deserved better treatment." Morgan made the bishop sit in the best chair and afterward he served the bishop food in golden plates. These were the best on the island. He also gave the bishop his own bedroom and told him that he would return him to Santa Marta and did not want any ransom (as his expedition had previously required). The bishop was surprised and could not believe what his eyes were seeing and his ears hearing.

"I thank you for these favors," the bishop stated.

"It's only justice," interrupted the pirate as he genuflected to the bishop.

"I beg you sir, do not send me back to Santa Marta," said the bishop.

"And why not?"

"I am now named the bishop of Panama and my church members in Santa Marta treated me with so much love that they did not want me to leave. If I am returned to Santa Marta I will have to go through the painful process of saying goodbye once more."

"If you please, sir, tell me where you want to go."

"To Cartagena. I would like to see Bishop Sanz Lozano. He was the one who ordained me and, as I am growing older, maybe I will never see him again in this world."

"It will be done as you order," said the pirate and he accompanied the bishop to his bedroom, which had been luxuriously prepared as well. He also presented the bishop with gifts. Before separating from the bishop Morgan said, "Maybe your Excellency did not expect to be treated as you deserve but I need to tell you the reason why."

"Was there a reason?" exclaimed the bishop. "I thought that your treatment was because of your good heart and I said to myself, how has this captain been so misrepresented? I was told that he was an enemy of the Spaniards and that he was very hard on them. I have found you as suave as a silk glove and more courteous than a Christian gentleman. Don't tell me, captain, that you had a motive for treating me as your friend. Please let me leave and I thank you as I would thank a son."

"Sir," said Morgan, kneeling before the bishop, "bless me, please bless me. Even though today I am called a heretic I have not always been one."

"Oh yes I will do it with all my heart," the bishop exclaimed, blessing the captain and being very moved. "Don't say that you are a heretic because you can cease to be one whenever you want to."

"No, no. That is" impossible, said the pirate. "But I will tell you the reason. My mother was an Irish Catholic who was kidnapped by a privateer named Mansfeld. She was married to my father who was part pirate, part farmer, and part contrabandist in the country of Wales. He belonged to the reformed religion. And how he ill treated her when she mentioned the word 'catholic'! So she resolved to hide her religion but not to forget it."

"Poor thing," exclaimed the bishop.

"My mother had me baptized by a Catholic priest and when I was a child she taught me to pray the prayers that she knew. As a boy my father sent me to be under the service of Mansfeld and I forgot what my mother had taught me."

"But you can remember it," said the bishop. "It is never too late to return to the right way."

"I repeat," said the pirate, "what has happened, has happened. Let's not talk about this anymore. The motive I have, then, for treating you as a friend and to have vengeance on the ones who ill treated you is because of my mother's memory. She died of a broken heart for which I am partially to blame."

Morgan was about to leave when the bishop called to him.

"What crimes are you going to punish? I don't remember any."

"What! Have you forgotten how they tied your hands and how they tormented you? How they hit you and how they brought you as a prisoner here against your will?"

"Yes, captain, I have forgotten it all and I have pardoned them from the bottom of my soul."

"You have forgiven them because you are a saint. But I am not one and I am going to punish them."

"Pardon them. For God's sake, pardon them. For the memory of your mother, pardon them!" exclaimed the bishop as he clasped his hands.

"For my mother's memory. Yes, it's going to be for my mother's memory." And saying this he left hastily.

"You will pardon them! Won't you please pardon them?" exclaimed the bishop, raising his voice.

After a few moments the bishop wanted to go outside and look for Morgan but he found all the doors locked from the outside. He had to go and lie down and rest because of his frayed nerves.

The first thing the next morning Morgan entered the room where the bishop was found kneeling in prayer before a crucifix. Morgan waited respectfully until Bishop Lucas Fernandez Piedrahita had finished praying. Then the bishop said good morning to his host.

"Look here," said Morgan, extending various luxurious ornaments. "I want to give you these small gifts for you to remember me."

The bishop looked at the gifts and said, "But those objects are not yours. Where did you get them?"

"I got them in Panama in the year 61," responded the pirate, "but I am just giving you things that actually belong to you. These were given to me as part of the treasure and I had kept them until I could dispose of them properly."

The bishop sighed and thanked the pirate. Morgan then ordered that the gifts be put in a box and that they should go on the ship with Piedrahita when he returned to Cartagena. While they were preparing the ship that would carry the bishop to Cartagena they continued conversing, the bishop and captain Morgan, since Morgan spoke Spanish fairly well. The bishop kept giving advice to which Morgan listened in silence but it probably made an impression on him. The next day Morgan was advised that the ship was ready to leave and Morgan accompanied the bishop to the port. The bishop raised his eyes in a very frightened manner as he saw four bodies swinging in the wind, hanging from gallows.

"Jesus," exclaimed the bishop. "What do I see there?"

"These are the bodies of those who mistreated you in Santa Marta," Morgan said coldly. "I hanged them last night as punishment."

"Didn't I ask you to pardon them?"

"Yes, but they were condemned to death already."

The bishop fell to his knees with his eyes full of tears and for a long time he prayed for those unfortunate people. He got up and said to the pirate, "You have made me suffer a lot and I will not be consoled until I know that you have abandoned the life of crime. I hope that these will be the last people that you kill."

When the vessel had left with the bishop, Morgan went to the fort and paced back and forth on top of the fort wall until the darkness of night hid the sailing ship from his vision. The bishop was received joyously in Cartagena then he was taken to his new post in Panama where he tried to rebuild the churches and monasteries of that city.

Two years later the bishop received a letter from Morgan himself which read:

"This is to advise your highness that I have pondered seriously what you told me before leaving for your country. I have decided to abandon my military career. I

have come to Jamaica under the protection of the governor and have married one of his daughters. I have also been knighted by the King of England, Charles II and for your good advice I want to express my gratitude.
Signed,
John Henry Morgan"

"Praise the Lord," exclaimed the bishop. "At least we have saved this soul from perpetual perdition." After this Morgan himself became the governor of Jamaica and ceased being a pirate.

This is a controversial story. There are some historians who deny that it ever happened but this author is supported by at least two reputable historians. First, Wenceslao Cabrera Ortiz, the great Colombian historian, in his book <u>San Andres y Providencia: A History</u>. Also it comes from the pen of Doña Soledad Acosta Samper. This story is also mentioned in the text book that was used when this author studied the history of Colombia.

The Search for Treasures

A few years ago, in the 1930s or 1940s, a well known citizen of San Andres decided that he was going to dig up Morgan's treasure. He saw some coins, but the demons chased him away so that he was not successful. It is believed, however, that from time to time some of the wealth was found.

In the middle of the nineteenth century a British sailing ship stopped in Providencia. They were in need of water and wood. Several members of the crew were sent ashore at Santa Catalina to obtain these items. The cook of the ship was named Curry. He was looking for wood with which to cook. He saw an iguana and tried to catch it but it ran into a hole. He tried to dig the iguana out of the hole but the dirt caved in around the hole which revealed a large trunk. The trunk contained gold bullion, coins, and jewels. Curry took as many of the coins as he could carry but the bullion was too heavy. Curry then went to find his companions to help him but when they returned they could not find the hole or the chest so the ship had to leave without the treasure. Upon arriving in England they informed the British admiralty which contacted the Colombian embassy and requested that the Colombian ambassador give permission to the British to obtain the treasure in Providencia and to share the proceeds. This was granted and so a British warship was sent to Santa Catalina to obtain the treasure but not a trace of gold, jewels, or even the trunk were found. And so the British government hanged Curry for his supposed failure and for deceiving the British and making them appear foolish. This happened when my grandfather was a boy.

In the first years of the twentieth century a man by the name of William Archbold had his hired men preparing a field for planting sugar cane on Santa Catalina. The dirt here also collapsed and revealed a chest which was rotting. The chest contained treasures consisting of gold coins and jewels. Mr. Archbold sent his workers home. He took the treasure and he became quite wealthy. He built a large house on the waterfront of Saint Isabel, the main port of Providencia. He also built a dock to accommodate the sailing vessels that came to Providencia.

As stated previously Morgan, the famous buccaneer, after his encounter with Monsignor Piedrahita of Santa Marta, left his criminal life, became the governor of Jamaica, and was knighted by the king of England. There are old cannons scattered over the surface of Providencia and Santa Catalina. One of them is found on Simeon Point at the entrance to Smooth Water Bay. Several years ago a man in Providencia, walking on the beach, looked in the mouth of the cannon and found a cloth bag which he was able to retrieve with some difficulty. This bag had also rotted but was filled with gold coins.

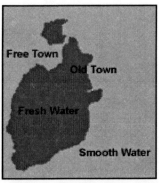

Map of Providence showing Smooth Water Bay

When I, Riva Robinson, and my siblings were growing up in old Providencia we were considered good, upright children and our playmates were supposed to be of the highest caliber. The Rudolph Newball family, brother Newball and his wife Elma, would not let their children associate with anyone except the Walter Robinson children. Lynd, their youngest son, asked his parents to ask my parents if I could spend the weekend with him at his home. This was granted.

Photo of Teacher Rudolph Newball with son Lynd and Wife, Elma

On Sunday afternoon Lynd and I walked from their house at Smooth Water Bay to Bottom House which is the next village. While walking along the road we saw two large stones. Each one had an iron bar stuck in it. The stones were covered with moss and dirt. I asked Lynd what these stones were. He said he did not know but they had always been there as far as he knew. When I went back home to Nellie Downs, which is on the other side of the island, I asked my father, Walter, what these particular stones meant. He stated that those stones were there ever since he was a boy. Sometime after this a chemist came to Providencia. He married a lady from Bottom House but the marriage did not last very long and the chemist left the island to go to Trinidad. Among his luggage were some very heavy boxes. The sailors loading them on the vessel wanted to know if these boxes were so heavy because they contained gold. Indeed this chemist became a very rich man and acquired extensive property, one of which was a hotel. In the meantime the people on Providencia noticed that these stones were missing.

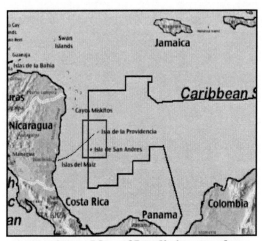

**Approximate Map of Lynd's journey from
Providencia past the Corn Islands (Islas del Maiz) to
Bluefields on the coast of Nicaragua**

Sometime after that weekend that I spent with Lynd, when
he was about 11 years old, his brother Harold came home on
vacation. This was in 1942. Harold worked on the Panama
Canal Zone. He came with his wife and baby daughter.
Friday afternoon Harold told Lynd, "Let's go fishing," so they
had a good time fishing near the reef. All too soon, the sun
started setting in the West and Harold told Lynd, "It's time to
go home." Just then a squall came up and tipped their boat
over. They managed to right it but they lost their paddles and
their sail. They tried to paddle the boat with their hands but
were making no headway. Harold saw an object in the water
which he thought was a piece of wood that they could use for
a paddle. Harold jumped overboard to catch the piece of wood
but he did not succeed in getting this object so he told Lynd he
was going to swim to shore to get help and that Lynd should
continue to bale the water out of the boat. Lynd lost sight of
Harold who was swimming towards shore to get help. But help
never came. The boat drifted beyond the end of the island and
Lynd laid down in the bottom of the boat and fell asleep.
When Lynd awoke the next morning there was no land in
sight, just waves and whitecaps. All that day he waited for
help and he became very thirsty by afternoon. It rained so he
was able to catch the rain water to drink. That night he again
laid down and went to sleep in the bottom of the boat. The
next morning, which was Sunday, he saw some vessels in the
distance and he took off his shirt and waved to them but they

did not see him because his boat was white, his shirt was white, and the tops of the waves were white. Also there were airplanes flying overhead during that day. The next day also there were airplanes flying overhead but they did not see him. Of course he was hungry and thirsty but it rained each afternoon so he got water to drink but no food. The next day it was calm and Lynd played with the water surrounding his boat. At that moment he heard a voice saying, "Look behind you." Then he saw a large shark turning his head on the side, ready to grab him. He slid down to the bottom of his boat and laid there for a long time. The next day he saw one large island, then one smaller. He also saw fishermen in their boats but they could not hear his shouts and, alas, his boat drifted past the islands. These were the Corn Islands of Nicaragua. The next day he saw no land but it rained that afternoon. The following day his boat drifted to land. He was quite weak by that time but he jumped out of the boat and tried to pull it up on the sand. He then saw some coco plum shrubs and he filled his stomach with the fruit. In about half an hour he had a terrible stomach ache. He saw a hut and walked up to it. There he met a man who was very surprised to see him. This man did not speak English but said to him in Spanish, "Where did you come from, boy?"

Lynd answered in English, "I've drifted from Providencia for a week. My canoe is right here on the beach. Come and I'll show it to you."

"That's impossible," he said, "the current won't allow a boat to touch land here."

The boat, of course, was gone, and had drifted away. The man partly carried and partly dragged Lynd to take him to Bluefields because he recognized that Lynd was very ill. Bluefields is the main sea port of Nicaragua on the Caribbean. There a telegram was sent to brother Newball, Lynd's father. Father and son had a bittersweet meeting in a few days because Lynd was alive and safe but Harold was never heard from. Lynd had prayed several times during his odyssey for God's protection. Lynd grew up to be an excellent physician with a specialty in oncology and he invented several cancer treatments.

Dr. Lynd Newball's hobby was searching for treasures. He even bought a Geiger counter and spent his vacations searching for treasure on Santa Catalina and Providencia but he never found any.

Not too long ago the Colombian navy sent a ship to Santa Catalina with divers who went into the previously mentioned cave but they allegedly only found some old rusted muskets. There is a possibility that others have found some treasure on these islands without making their findings known. Just in the past few years an Italian company was excavating to build the second largest hotel on San Andres which was located on the hill just above the town of San Luis. They found a treasure, the size of which was not disclosed. There might still be some pirate treasure waiting to be found. Reader, will it be you?

Re-Colonizing

The pirate activity continued in the Caribbean until the first part of the nineteenth century. Spain and England would take turns in governing the islands and were fighting back and forth for control. Towards the end of the seventeenth century the importance of the islands dwindled. After 1688 both the British and the Spanish lost interest in the islands and the population decreased immensely, so much so that some historians have stated that the islands were uninhabited. I do not believe this to be true. They were never completely uninhabited which has also been stated by other historians and the islanders themselves. The people that were living on the islands would hide in the interior of the islands whenever a ship appeared. The people on San Andres would hide on the hill. The people on Providencia would hide in the area of Split Hill.

In the mid-1700s the islands started to be recolonized. People came to the islands from Europe, especially England, Scotland, Holland, France, and Spain. Some came from other parts of the Caribbean, especially Jamaica. A few came from Central America and from North America.

It might be said that until 1830 Providencia was the more important of the two islands and the archipelago was governed from Providencia. In 1833 the seat of government was changed to San Andres. Providencia was easier to defend militarily but when San Andres, the larger island, became more populous, the importance shifted.

In the 1700s, slaves were introduced, especially on San Andres. Some were brought from Jamaica, some directly from West Africa, and some were bought from the Spaniards. Over time, the number of slaves on San Andres was greatly increased. Many of these slaves would take the names of their masters, especially if their masters were kind to them. There was mingling of the races, minimally at first, but slowly increasing after slavery was abolished. Because of the increased population of slaves on San Andres, by the twentieth century ninety percent of the population of that island was black. Because of this there were more blacks on San Andres than on Providencia.

In 1780 Captain Stephen Kemble, captain of a British ship, took refuge from a storm in San Andres. In his description of his voyage he stated that he found twelve families on the island, the majority being mulattos. He also stated that they were raising cattle and growing cotton as the chief crop.

Cotton became the principal crop, especially in San Andres with up to 200 metric tons of cotton being exported each year. The highest grade of cotton, which was grown on San Andres and Providencia, was called Sea Island Cotton and this was preferred above any other cotton grown in the Caribbean. Several people owned relatively large plantations.

Some British citizens living on the islands requested land grants from the Spanish government with the condition of becoming Spanish subjects and to be converted to the Catholic religion. This they did only in name. This business was done with the assistance of the Irishman Lieutenant Thomas O'Neille. Actually, O'Neille's parents were Irish but he was born on the Canary Islands so he spoke both Spanish and English fluently. He was highly respected by both the Spaniards and the Islanders. He became governor on several occasions of the Islands and the Spanish colonies on the coast of Central America. He came to San Andres on a Spanish ship as translator but because of his knowledge of both English and Spanish he was able to negotiate decisions that favored the Islanders. The Spaniards wanted to put into effect the treaty of Versailles of 1783 which, in part, stated that all English speaking people should be evacuated from the islands. A ship was sent to evacuate the islands in 1789 but because of Lieutenant O'Neille this did not happen.

Captain Francis Archbold

Captain Francis Archbold was one who brought slaves directly from Africa to the Caribbean, including Jamaica and Providencia. Archbold was a Scotsman. Captain Archbold obtained a land grant from the Spanish government on the island of Providencia. This was under the condition that he become a Spanish citizen. He did this but never acted as such. He always remained a Britisher in actuality. With the help of Lieutenant Thomas O'Neille, who was the governor of the archipelago of the islands of San Andres and Providencia, Captain Archbold became the principal land owner on the island of Providencia. Captain Archbold first lived in Jamaica with his wife. They had a daughter, Mary, but Archbold's wife died in giving birth to Mary in 1785. It was in 1787 that Francis Archbold received the land grant from the Spanish government to settle in Bottom House in Providencia. It was with this slave trader that the reoccupation of Providencia began once more in earnest. In 1788 Archbold moved to Providencia, taking Mary with him. Mary was three years old at the time. He also brought with him several slaves that he himself had brought directly from Africa. He cultivated a large amount of land that he had received in the Spanish grant. Several different fruits and vegetables were grown but the chief crop was cotton. The slaves were very handy for the cultivation of cotton. On Providencia Captain Archbold sired six more children, three males and three females. The males were James, Pierce, and Francis Caldwell, Jr. Today the Archbold family is the largest on Providencia as well as one of the most numerous on San Andres.

Chapter 2: The Introduction of Christianity in the 1800s

The Livingston Clan

Captain Archbold became a friend of Philip Beeckman Livingston, Sr. who originally was a Scotsman who settled in the British colonies of North America. When the United States of America was formed Livingston remained a loyalist. He traveled extensively and finally settled in Providencia. Livingston also obtained a land grant in Providencia and between him and Captain Archbold owned most of the land on that island. Philip Livingston married Captain Archbold's daughter Mary. At first the Livingstons lived in Jamaica but then they moved to Providencia and lived on Philip's large estate. Livingston had obtained his land grant from the Spanish with the help of Thomas O'Neille. Livingston farmed extensively employing slaves brought from Africa by Captain Archbold. Philip Beeckman Livingston Sr. was mayor in the era when Luis Aury captured Providencia.

Photo of Philip Beeckman Livingston, Jr.

Philip and Mary Livingston had several children, the eldest a son named Philip Beeckman Livingston, Jr., born January 16, 1814. Philip Beeckman Livingston, Jr., spent his childhood in Providencia in the area of Bottom House. The family then moved to Jamaica for Philip Jr.'s education. After his education, Philip, Jr. was on a ship as an apprentice for five years. On one trip, his ship, traveling from England, stopped in Kingston, Jamaica. Philip heard that his mother was in Kingston at that time. He requested to the captain to be given leave so that he could see his mother. His request was denied several times. On the night the ship sailed Philip abandoned the ship. The captain hired another man to take Philip's place. Two days later the ship wrecked on a reef on the western end of Jamaica and all on board perished.

Mary, Philip Jr.'s mother, sent him, her eldest son, to Providencia to manage their property there, to free the slaves that the Livingston family owned, and to divide the land between them and himself. He left Jamaica in March of 1834 on a ship going to San Andres where he stayed several days with the Bowie family, a British family who owned extensive property as well as slaves. While staying with the Bowies young Philip met and got acquainted with 17 year old Ann Eliza O'Neille, daughter of Governor Thomas O'Neille. Philip then continued his trip to Providencia with Ann Eliza on his mind.

On August 1, 1834, he conferred absolute freedom to all of his family's slaves in Providencia and divided the land among them, keeping a share for himself. The freed slaves kept the name of their master so that today Livingston is the surname of a large number of the people in Bottom House.

Philip's romance with Ann Eliza continued for the next five years after which they were married by the governor of the archipelago, Antonio Escalona, in San Andres. Why in San Andres and not in Providencia will be explained later. Philip and Ann Eliza decided to live on Providencia but Ann Eliza soon missed her parents in San Andres so she and Philip moved to that island. Before his marriage to Ann Eliza, Philip had two illegitimate children born to an islander. Philip and Ann Eliza reared these children.

Philip freed the slaves the family owned in San Andres on August 1, 1838. In the fall of 1844 Philip traveled to the United States of America. There he attended a series of religious meetings in Oberlin, Ohio held by a Reverend Cook. Philip was baptized in Lake Erie after being converted. Later Philip was baptized again by Baptist minister Reverend

William W. Evarts and became a Baptist. Philip was licensed to preach on January 1, 1845.

When he set foot on San Andres he was 31. Philip Beeckman Livingston Jr., was 5'5" tall and weighed 130 pounds with a light complexion and blue eyes. This was the beginning of Christianity on the archipelago of San Andres and Providencia. Before this there was no religion on the islands but by 1890, through the work of Philip, ninety-five percent of the people on San Andres and Providencia professed the Baptist faith.

After Livingston freed his family's slaves he worked tirelessly with the other slave owners to free their slaves but with poor success. Slavery was officially abolished by the government of Colombia in 1851. Not everyone on San Andres complied. Pastor Livingston corresponded with the government in Bogota, the capital of Colombia, and by 1853 the government abolished slavery everywhere. Even then slavery continued sporadically. For example, in the latter part of the 1850s my great grandmother, Eudosia McKeller Robinson, bequeathed her slaves to her daughter, Ada Robinson. Of course, Ada being a young girl at that time, said, 'I don't want any slaves.' So the slaves were freed.

Pastor Philip Beeckman Livingston, Jr.., was the main force behind not only establishing the Baptist Christianity on San Andres and Providencia but also the abolishing of slavery on the islands.

About that time Ann Eliza's health started to fail and on July 2, 1862, she died. She and Philip had been married for 23 years. The Livingstons had a housekeeper, Miss Josephine Pomaire. Josephine tenderly cared for Ann Eliza during her illness. Josephine was a black woman, a descendant of slaves on San Andres. She lived in the home of Pastor Livingston and his family after the death of Ann Eliza and continued to work in the Livingston home, caring for the children, the house, and cooking. Three years after Ann Eliza's death Pastor Livingston took Josephine to the office of Mayor John Smith, who married them. If anything could catch on faster than a revival in a Baptist church it would be a scandal. Many people accused the pastor of not being respectful to his deceased wife's memory by marrying Josephine so soon after Ann Eliza's death. The white people considered it improper for him to have married a black woman. The commotion continued for several weeks. Then Pastor Livingston had enough. On Sunday morning he appeared in the pulpit with his rifle and laid it in front of him. Before beginning his sermon he said that he had willingly married Josephine and that was his own business. He ordered that the gossip stop. It did. On January 1, 1867, a son was born to this union who was named Brockholst. Pastor Philip taught his son, Brockholst, everything he knew. He tried to send him to get educated in the United States of America but because of his dark color he was not accepted in any of the U.S. universities so his son's entire education was given him by his father.

Pastor Philip Beeckman Livingston Jr., on August 29, 1891 died of natural causes. He was the person most responsible for bringing Christianity to the archipelago of San Andres and Providencia. At his death, 95% of the people on these islands professed the Baptist faith.

Picture of Brockholst Livingston

Brockholst Livingston was six feet tall, heavy set, dark skinned, round faced, with black hair and brown eyes. At 17 years of age he married Ethel Forbes, a native of San Andres. The Forbes had lived on the island for generations.
Brockholst was called by the people "Mr. B, our native son." His father taught him medicine and he became an

30

outstanding surgeon. He brought medical books, medicines, and surgical instruments from the United States. Since by that time ether had been invented, he could perform surgery without having to give whiskey to patients until they became unconscious as his father used to do. Pastor Brockholst was the most influential man on San Andres during his lifetime. He was pastor, delivered babies, cared for the sick, performed marriages, granted divorces, and buried the dead. He owned considerable land and maintained the dock and warehouse at Haine Bite. The family schooner, the Vicson was administered by him. When the government officials did not perform correctly he denounced them from the pulpit. Everyone feared and respected him. His word was law. Brockholst and Ethel had two sons, Philip Beeckman III and Thomas Brockholst.

Baptist Church on the Hill, San Andres

Brockholst was an eloquent preacher with a big voice. One of his major projects was to build the church which still stands today on May Mount. The building was fifty feet wide, seventy-five feet long, and seated a thousand people. Brockholst traveled to Mobile, Alabama where he hired an architect and stayed there until the building was constructed, then dismantled, and shipped to San Andres where it was reassembled, a remarkable feat indeed. Due to the efforts of the Pastors Philip Beeckman and Brockholst, over 90% of the people could read and write. The people were economically sound and law abiding. There was no jail nor was one needed. Stealing was practically unknown. Locks were not to be seen

31

on the doors and even the stores in North End were closed at night and on Sundays without being locked. At the time almost everyone attended church on Sundays. Like Pastor Philip Beeckman, Pastor Brockholst did not limit the ministry to San Andres. They organized the church in Providencia also. William J. Davidson was ordained as the first pastor of the Baptist church in Providencia. Other pastors were Simon Howard, Francis Caldwell Archbold, Simon Howard, Jr., and others who served over the years. Pastor Brockholst sent his sons, Philip Beeckman III and Thomas Brockholst, to school in Jamaica after they had finished their primary education in San Andres. At first the plan was for Philip to be the minister and Tom to study medicine. After the first year Philip changed to medicine and Thomas took theology, being more spiritual and Philip more interested in the human body, demonstrated by the pictures he had taken of the pretty Jamaican girls. The boys, after high school, went to Howard University in Washington, D.C. Pastor Brockholst, in early 1911 developed a tumor in the back of his neck. After several surgeries it would return each time. He finally died on August 8, 1911. Pastor Brockholst Livingston Pomaire was a great man who, like his father, was successful in the advancement of the Baptist church and in the progress of the islands of San Andres and Providencia. A greater funeral was never held on San Andres, neither before or since. At Pastor Brockholst's burial his son Thomas gave the funeral address.

A problem of the islands that both Philip Beeckman and Brockholst had to confront was superstition, the belief in obeah and duppies. Obeah is the practice of magic. It is supposed to work upon someone for good or for evil, mostly evil, placing a curse on the person. An obeah man is a specialist in the working of obeah so that when someone wanted harm to be done to a person or persons he would solicit the services of the obeah man. Duppy is a spirit, usually the spirit of the dead. It was believed that a duppy is able to aid or to harm the living. A duppy is a ghost. The superstitions of the people were a constant concern of the Livingston pastors and they seemed unable to stamp it out. In order to keep the spirit away from babies, a Bible and a pair of scissors were placed at the head of the crib, under the pillow.

If a person died on a rainy day it was believed that that dead person was crying. There was such fear of the spirit of the dead that when someone died babies were handed from one side of the coffin to the next so that the spirit would not molest the infant. When the body of the deceased was being carried in front of a home the window shutters were shut. When someone died the bereaved family would select a person called a 'circular' who would ride on horseback around the island announcing the death and the funeral plans. When someone died, before and during the burial, almost invariably someone would engage in sterics, a trance like state in which a person would appear to convulse, faint, shriek loudly, or even pass out overcome with emotions. During the night there would be a set up lasting all night during which the mourners would eat and drink food prepared usually by the family of the dead person. There would be the singing of hymns all night also.

The missionaries, both Baptist and Seventh day Adventist, had to deal with spiritualistic activities. Here are three stories that I heard or experienced when I was growing up.

There was a man in San Andres named Stunu. Stunu was a man of average size but he had a reputation of being able to eat enormous quantities of food. He would make bets about this where he would apparently eat a full stalk of bananas by himself or he would eat twelve loaves of bread or two large cans of pilot bread biscuits. He would do this demonstration often but it was finally found out that if you went to his house afterwards the things that he had apparently eaten were found in his house.

There was a doctor by the name of Dr. Hemmans who, after several years of practice in San Andres, died. His wife was approached by a man by the name Carlos who wanted to buy a part of her property because it adjoined his. She refused. Afterward she would see fire in her house or when she made bread, the bread would walk out of the oven in her plain sight.

There was also a man in Providencia. His name was Watson. Watson was a very good school teacher but after a while he started making spiritualistic demonstrations. He would apparently change himself into a pig and be walking around and grunting like a pig. For all intents and purposes he was a pig. One night Roosevelt Robinson took several stones and hit the pig. The pig said, "It is I, Watson, please don't hit me anymore." The next morning Watson could not get out of bed because he was so bruised. These were some of the things that the missionaries had to deal with.

After burying their father, both Philip III and Thomas Livingston returned to the United States to continue their education. The next summer Thomas returned to San Andres with his bride, Julia Allen, a theological degree, and two trunks full of books. He had been ordained to the ministry by the Berean Baptist Church in Washington D.C. Tom was an eloquent preacher whose sermons nobody wanted to miss. The next year Philip III graduated from the school of medicine of Loyola University in Chicago. He returned to establish a medical practice in his island home. He had married an American nurse, Miss Suzanna Smith. His freight included the latest surgical instruments, medicines, a house full of furniture, a new Dodge car, and a pool table.

Photo of Thomas Livingston

There were a group of members who did not agree with the policies and the changes that Pastor Thomas had established. He had difficulty with the more conservative deacons in the church. The church members in North End rejected Thomas's ideas. Deacon James Manoah Smith was the principal leader of the group. The North End group declared themselves to be a separate church. James Smith was sent to Colon to discuss affiliation with the Christian Mission Church of Panama. This was worked out and in 1915 this group adopted the name of Christian Mission Church of

Panama in San Andres but locally they called themselves the Christian Mission Church. This church was pastored by James Manoah Smith until his death in 1930. The Christian Mission Church and the Baptists maintained cordial relations. The doctrines of both churches were identical and they collaborated in ordinations and funerals and the pastors exchanged pulpits from time to time.

Meanwhile, Dr. Philip III's wife, Suzy, left him, secured a divorce, and returned to what she considered a better life in the USA. Julia then talked Tom into returning to the United States. In 1922 he resigned as pastor of the church and he too returned to the United States. The church in San Andres was left in the hands of Ricaute Howard, Wallace Hayes, and the other deacons. This brought to an end the seventy-five year period of the gospel being preached and the Baptist church being established in the islands by the Livingston clan. These islands owe a great debt of gratitude to the Livingstons. All of us islanders should not forget what Philip Beeckman Livingston, Jr., Brockholst Livingston Pomaire, and Thomas Livingston Forbes, have contributed to the overall progress of the archipelago.

For four years after Thomas Livingston resigned as pastor of the Baptist church in San Andres and returned to the USA the church was directed by the board of deacons. Then the board of deacons asked Reverend Nigard, a missionary who was in Cartagena, to assist them in getting a pastor. Reverend Nigard got in touch with the home mission board of the American Baptist Convention of the United States.

The mission extended an invitation to the Reverend Dr. Noel Julian La Rosa Gonsalves of British Guyana originally, who now was pastor of the First Baptist Church of Lexington, Virginia, to become pastor of the Baptist church in San Andres. Pastor Gonsalves and his wife, after praying and discussing the matter, accepted in June of 1926. They took a steam ship to Panama. The Gonsalves had no children. Deacon Wallace Hayes was sent to Panama to help the Gonsalves in getting to San Andres. The next day the pastor and his wife were taken to the port in Colon to embark to the island. After traveling to Panama on a large passenger ship they were unprepared and shocked to see The Bird, a sailing sloop of about 30 tons, to which they were to entrust their lives for the next three days. After what seemed to be an eternity enduring sea sickness the Gonsalves, the distressed pair, heard what they thought to be good news: "Land ahoy," only to find out that they were passing South Southwest Key and had more than three hours before arriving at the port in San Andres.

Photo of Pastor Gonsalves

Once in San Andres the Gonsalves were made welcome and comfortable by the aged mother of deacon Wallace Hayes. The next few days islanders poured into their house to welcome them with gifts of chickens, eggs, plantains, cassava, bananas, and other things to show their love to Pastor Gonsalves. Pastor Gonsalves found the church in need of repair. With no money in the treasury and the membership of several hundred that reverend Thomas Livingston had left had dwindled to about fifty. An intensive program of evangelization was started immediately. When the initial evangelization period ended after several weeks the church role numbered 550.

Catholicism in the Islands
The Catholic church started its work in the archipelago of San Andres and Providencia in a more or less organized fashion in 1902 when the first missionary priest of the Josephite order was sent to Providencia. The first priest was

Albert Strobelli at the ripe old age of seventy. At first Father
Strobelli was met with a cool reception. This was obvious
since 95% of the islanders were Baptist. Father Strobelli soon
found a supporter in Pastor Eusebio Howard who had split
against his brother as pastors of the Saint Isabel Baptist
church. Eusebio had started a church in Comsi, Providencia
but was then converted to Catholicism and turned over his
church to Father Strobelli. A second Catholic church was
started in the area of Bailey by Father Timothy St. John.
These Josephite priests had their headquarters in Baltimore.
Under the Josephite priests the Catholic church increased
rapidly and by 1912 there were 300 Catholics on Providencia.
The success of Catholicism under the Josephites was due in no
small part to the general attitude of these Josephite
missionaries who were friendly and showed respect and
tolerance to the customs and values of the native island
people. These priests spoke English and maintained cordial
relations with the Baptists and the Seventh day Adventists.
They even attended special religious services of the
Protestants whenever invited. The Josephite priests were well
liked and when the time came for them to leave there was a
great deal of sadness among the people of Providencia who
had grown to accept and admire them. The departure of these
American Josephites came as a result of the political conflicts
that had developed between the United States and Colombia
over the loss of Panama. Colombia had become increasingly
suspicious of U.S. intentions and therefore all Americans,
including the Josephite missionaries, were suspect.

The Colombian government negotiated with the Saint
Joseph Missionary Society in Middle Hill, England, to take
over the Catholic mission in Providencia. In 1912, after the
American priests had departed, Father James Fitzpatrick,
Father Herbert Keane, and Father Richard Turner came.
Others came later. The Middle Hill priests stayed until 1926.
The Catholic Church was more successful during this period
in Providencia and there were Catholic churches in several
areas. In San Andres there was only one small church. The
Middle Hill priests saw their mission as limited to the
conversion of souls to Catholicism and were in no way
interested in forcing a cultural change on the people. In fact,
the Middle Hill priests were very much at home with the
island people who not only spoke English but who manifested
an Anglo Saxon way of looking at the world and claimed to be
descendants of English, Irish, and Scottish ancestors. It was
difficult for the islanders to see much difference between the

Catholic and Baptist churches. The Catholics had midweek prayer meetings and often they sang hymns from the Baptist hymnal. The priests preached sermons and prayed for the sick just like the Baptists did.

Starting in 1927 the Josephite priests were replaced by Spanish speaking priests of the Capuchin order based in Valencia, Spain. The Colombian government wanted to bring about the complete Colombianization of San Andres and Providencia. This meant that all islanders would speak only Spanish, become Catholics, abandon the island culture, and accept the culture of the continentals. The first group of Capuchin priests were Father Cristobal Canales, Father David Castlefort, Father Carlos Orihuela, and Father Eugenio Carcagente who served as their superior. The Josephite priests had made their headquarters in Providencia whereas the Capuchins settled in San Andres. Colombia had signed a concordat with the Vatican and about 1927 the government considered that the Colombianization of the archipelago was proceeding too slowly. Then the Colombian government proceeded to impose the provisions of the concordat on the islanders which stated that all missionary activity in certain parts of Colombia should only be done by the Catholic Church. The islands of San Andres, Providencia, and Santa Catalina were included.

The Capuchin order was the perfect instrument for the Colombian government to carry out the Colombianization process in the islands. The Capuchin order was at first to destroy the native cultural foundations and replace them with what they considered true civilization. That was based on Iberian customs, traditions, the Spanish language, and the Catholic religion. Ultimately the intentions of the Capuchins were to completely eradicate all forms of Protestantism. Their goal was to transform the people of those islands into 'real Colombians' who spoke only Spanish and were Catholics. With considerable funds from the government of Colombia a vigorous program of building schools and other facilities was begun by the Intendente. Jobs on the construction were granted only to Catholics. Because of the poverty, due largely to the failure of the main industry of the islands which was the exportation of coconuts, many of the Baptists joined the Catholic church to get government employment. These were called 'job Catholics' by the general population of the islands.

As stated above, the Baptists, under Pastor Gonsalves, were a success. The momentum gained by the Baptist congregation did not go unnoticed by the emerging Roman

Catholic mission. The momentum of the Baptist church displeased the Catholic mission and Pastor Gonsalves was charged with speaking against the Catholic church and with speaking against the nuns. Two local lawyers defended Pastor Gonsalves. They were Dr. Lever and Dr. Simon Howard. The attorneys succeeded in having the case dropped and Pastor Gonsalves was exonerated without having to go to court. There were several other times when pastor Gonsalves was accused of breaking the law but he was well defended by Dr. Simon Howard.

Poison in the Drink

The 20th of July is the celebration of Colombian independence from Spain. On the 7th of August Colombians celebrate their complete freedom which was sealed at the battle of Boyaca. On San Andres the custom is to celebrate the events of August at San Luis rather than North End, which is the center of festivities for the 20th of July. Pastor Gonsalves was invited to be one of the speakers in San Luis. The other was Dr. Simon Howard. Pastor Gonsalves accepted and prepared his address. He entitled it "The Forward March of Democracy." On this special holiday a large crowd gathered, including the Intendente Tadeo Lozano, his wife, and several government officials. Dr. Howard gave his speech first. Then Pastor Gonsalves gave a 15 minute presentation. The patriotic emotion of the crowd exploded with loud prolonged applause as Pastor Gonsalves ended his speech with the words "As you gaze on the red, which typifies the bloodshed for Colombian independence, remember that says to you
'be brave.' Long live the sovereign republic of Colombia."
Before the applause died down Intendente Tadeo Lozano invited Pastor Gonsalves to accompany him to the banquet hall. They entered together. Around the large table were seated distinguished guests. Tadeo Lozano took his seat at the head of the table. Next to him sat his wife. Gonsalves was given the next seat. The glasses had been filled with wine in advance. The Intendente then arose and in a very dignified manner proposed a toast to the President and the health of the nation. The glasses were lifted in unison. Pastor Gonsalves raised his glass along with everyone else but did not drink the wine. At this, Intendente Lozano became enraged and blurted out, "What sort of foolish religion is this that you cannot drink to the health of the President of the republic?" Calmly Gonsalves replied that he was sorry but he did not drink wine, not even at home. The doctor seated next to Pastor Gonsalves,

wishing to reduce the tension said, "That is all right. I will drink it for him." He then gulped the contents of the glass and sat down. In a few moments the doctor uttered a shriek and fell to the floor, screaming, and had a convulsion. He was given an antidote by Dr. Philip Beeckman Livingston III, who was present. He hung between life and death for three weeks, but lived. In the commotion that broke out, Pastor Gonsalves slipped out and was driven to his home by his chauffer. It was never known who put the poison in the Pastor's glass.

After Pastor Gonsalves served in San Andres for one year, he became fatigued, probably due to the many problems he had with the Capuchin priests and with the government. He left for a vacation to British Guyana where he and his wife stayed for eight months. In the meantime he received many letters from San Andres urging him to return. He got a visa in Port of Spain, Trinidad, and then sailed to Colon, Panama. There they tried to get a vessel going to San Andres but the captains of the vessels going to San Andres refused to give them passage saying that they were threatened with a fine of $200 if they took the pastor to the island. For a month they remained in Colon, discouraged. Then the tide turned. Captain Martinez arrived with the schooner Peabody which he owned along with Arthur May. These two men were probably the two most wealthy men on San Andres. Mr. Arthur May told Captain Martinez to take the pastor back to San Andres at all costs. Martinez assured the Gonsalves that the Peabody was worth $25,000 and that they were willing to risk losing the ship to take him to the island. The Gonsalves boarded the schooner awaiting the time of departure. A Panamanian official came on board with orders to remove Pastor Gonsalves from the vessel because he had interfered with the internal affairs of the archipelago. The one who saved the day was the daughter of Captain Martinez who, with waving arms and flying hair, verbally attacked the officer in a tirade of Spanish. The official became so confused that he hastily retreated to the safety of the dock. Thirty-eight hours later they arrived in San Andres and because of the powerful influence of Martinez and May no fine was levied. Upon arriving on The Hill the Pastor and his wife were surprised to see a brand new two story parsonage. Pastor Gonsalves served the Baptist church for about twenty years, and then retired.

The Coconut Plague

During the latter part of the eighteenth century and in the early part of the nineteenth century, the principal crop of the islands was cotton. Around 1850 several land owners started to plant coconut palms, anticipating that with the freeing of the slaves cotton would no longer be profitable. By 1860 San Andres had become one large coconut plantation. The exporting of coconuts became the chief industry of the islands. As many as 30 million coconuts were exported annually.

Up to the twentieth century it was prohibited to lay people by the Catholic church to read the Bible. The non-Catholic churches on the islands were accused of teaching Christianity out of the King James Version of the Bible which was considered to be incomplete and full of errors. Furthermore, it was taught that only priests had the knowledge and the authority to read and teach the scriptures. The nuns of the San Luis Catholic school decided that they would take matters into their own hands. They informed the students that they were going to begin a Bible study the next day and that each student should bring their family Bible to school the next morning. The nuns prepared a table and covered it with a table cloth. All the Bibles were placed on the table as the students entered. After all were seated the teachers tied the four corners of the table cloth together, and then carried the Bibles outside. Kerosene was poured on them then they were ignited. The children started to cry. Soon the news of what was done spread over
the whole island. Many protests followed. It is generally stated by the islanders to this day that in a few days after the burning the coconut palm under which the Bibles were burned became infected with a plague and died. This disease spread and almost all of the coconut palms on the island became infected. Two years after the burning of the Bibles 90% of the coconut trees had died. It became necessary to replant all the farms on the island. The economy of the islands was very adversely affected by this loss. By the early 1940s the harvest of coconuts was up to 15 million. This was half as much as in the 1920s.

My own family suffered loss. The Robinsons had recently purchased the 65 ton schooner Klondike which was used in exporting coconuts to Cartagena but this vessel had to be sold when there were no more coconuts.

Many islanders believed this tragic event was the result of a curse from God.

Chapter 3—Adventurers and Politicians

Luis Aury

Colombia declared its independence from Spain on July 20, 1810, but its freedom from Spain was not secured until nine years later in the battle of Boyaca on August 7, 1819. During this period the islands retained their sympathy with Spain at first especially since they got very little news about what was happening on the continent. In 1818 French adventurer Luis Aury captured the island of Providencia. He had at his command 14 ships and 800 men. Two months later his troops were bolstered by the arrival of a British ship with 150 more from Jamaica. In 1819 Gregor McGregor arrived with 394 more men to join Aury. Aury offered his services to Simon Bolivar and wanted to be the head of the navy but Bolivar chose Brion to be the head of the navy and told Aury in no uncertain terms that he did not need the services of a bandit. Aury was in command of the island of Providencia until August 30, 1821, when he accidentally fell off his horse, hitting his head, and died.

During this time the mayor of Providencia was Philip Beeckman Livingston, Sr. Colonel Jean Baptiste Faquaire assumed command after Aury's unfortunate accident. In 1822 the people of Providencia requested and signed their allegiance to Colombia. Seventeen people signed the document but only 6 were from Providence: Pedro Archbold, James Archbold, Francis Archbold, Ralph McBean, Jack McKellar, and James Davidson. The others were military men. The ones from San Andres who signed were: Torquel Bowie, Thomas O'Nielle, Peter Peterson, George Barker, William Lever, and Max Ogle May. Those who signed from Corn Island were Max Ogle May and Benjamin Downs. The archipelago was governed after Aury's death by Faquaire. The islands were incorporated into the Gran Colombia. Faquaire's position was ratified by General Santander, the Vice President of the country.

At this time the title of governor was changed to prefect. In 1824 the new prefect was Antonio Cardenas who was in office until 1833. At this time Panama and the Miskito Coast of Central America belonged to Colombia but none of these governors did anything to advance the sovereignty of Colombia over the Miskito Coast. The country as a whole neglected completely its territories. The islands of San Andres, Providencia, Santa Catalina, and Corn Island and the

Miskito Coast were connected culturally and even by families but they were neglected by the mother country. Several families were divided so that some part of the family would be from Providencia or San Andres and the other part of the family would live in Corn Island or Bluefields. For example, the Brittons and the Downs were examples of this division.

Cardenas transferred the seat of government from Providencia to San Andres because this island was more populous. Cardenas was named to govern not only San Andres and Providencia but also Corn Island and all of the Miskito Coast of Central America. All of these formed part of Colombian territory. This area was all part of the viceroyalty of New Granada under Spain and so became part of Colombia when Bolivar freed the area from Spain. Cardenas paid no attention to Colombian interests other than in San Andres and Providencia.

Cardenas was replaced as governor by Antonio Escalona who governed from 1833 to 1845. When Escalona traveled from Cartagena to San Andres he was afraid of encountering bad weather. This is exactly what he got. He became terribly seasick. High waves dashed over the deck and the ship continually listed to one side. The other passengers were also seasick and a terrible odor was coming from the cabins. Commander Escalona had never experienced anything like this. His empty stomach was tied up in knots from so much vomiting. Finally reaching port in San Andres he swore that he would never again board a ship as long as he lived. And he didn't. The result of this decision would prove unfortunate to the interests of Colombia not only in the archipelago but--in all of the Colombian territories in Central America. Antonio Escalona never visited Providencia, Corn Island, or the Miskito Coast.

We previously noted that Philip Beeckman Livingston married Ann Eliza O'Nielle. Philip's home was in Providencia and he intended to continue living there. Antonio Escalona was to perform the marriage ceremony but he would not get on a ship to travel to Providencia so Philip and Ann Eliza were married in San Andres by Governor Escalona. They then settled in Providencia until Ann Eliza got home sick and they moved to San Andres. Escalona changed the name of the Gaugh (a town in San Andres) to San Luis de Providencia and in his reports to Bogota acted as if this was Corn Island and the Miskito Coast. The islands complained to Bogota. At first the government paid no attention but finally an investigation was made. Escalona knew that he was going to be deposed and so he committed suicide, shooting himself in the head. This was the way his promise of never getting on a ship again was kept.

Colombian Territories Lost

Simon Bolivar's dream was to have a country in Latin America large enough and great enough to rival the great country of the North, the United States of America. This is why The Great Colombia was formed. The Great Colombia consisted of Colombia, Venezuela, Ecuador, Panama, and the Central American territories of the Miskito Coast, which is now Nicaragua, and the archipelago of San Andres, Providencia, and the Corn Islands. Bolivar intended to add to Colombia what is now Peru and Bolivia. But this dream never became a reality.

There were several factors that caused the loss of Colombian territory. There was the rebellion of General Paez leading to the separation of Venezuela. Then Ecuador separated from Colombia because of the capricious dealings of Marshall Sucre. There were several civil wars in Colombia itself; there was the carelessness of the island governors appointed by the government of the Republic, as previously stated. The first governors were called prefects, the first of which was Antonio Cardenas who governed for seven years, then was replaced in 1833 by Antonio Escalona. These prefects did not care for the Colombian interest in Corn Island or on the Miskito Coast. These areas were part of the territory over which these governors were appointed to administrate and govern. During the remainder of the nineteenth century as well as the early parts of the twentieth century, Colombia did very little to preserve its territorial integrity. Whatever navy Colombia had during this period disintegrated. Colombia made only weak diplomatic efforts to preserve its territorial integrity. In spite of this several countries including Great Britain recognized Colombian sovereignty over the Miskito Coast and its Caribbean Islands. But Nicaragua also laid claim over all the Miskito Coast and the Corn Islands as well as San Andres and Providencia.

Panama, the Canal, and Separation from Colombia

The people of Panama were displeased with the mother country because they were not considered as a fully fledged department but only as a territory. About 1879 Colombia made negotiations with the French company headed by Ferdinand de Lesseps to build a canal across the isthmus of

Panama. De Lesseps had built the Suez Canal which was officially opened November 27, 1869. The Suez Canal was a success in spite of the British opposition. The Panama Canal Company was then created. This canal was to be without locks just as the Suez Canal had been. De Lesseps was appointed president of the company. The decision was to build the canal at sea level without locks. De Lesseps went to Panama in 1880. He estimated that it would take eight years to build this canal and that it would cost 650 million francs. Work on the canal was started in 1882, however the technical difficulties of operating in the wet tropics of Panama made the project a very difficult one. Particularly disastrous were the recurrent landslides into the excavations from the bordering water saturated heights as well as the death toll from malaria and yellow fever. These things hampered the progress of the project and in the end insufficient funds and corruption ended the project. The Panama Canal Company declared bankruptcy in December of 1888.

In 1904 the United States of America bought out the assets of the French company and started to work under a revised plan. Meanwhile Colombia and the United States of America started negotiations to build a canal but Colombia broke off negotiations because Colombia thought the terms were too one-sided, in favor of the United States of America. On various occasions different sites were suggested for the building of the canal. Among others there was one suggested across Nicaragua crossing the lake near Managua and using also the San Juan River. Another area under consideration was on the eastern border of Panama with Colombia using the Atrato River. On June 28, 1902, the congress of the United States of America authorized approval for the construction of the Panama Canal. Then on November 3, 1903, Panama declared its independence from Colombia and with the help of the United States achieved its separation. This was under the gunboat diplomacy of Theodore Roosevelt.

At this time the American warship Nashville, under direct orders from Theodore Roosevelt, came to San Andres bringing two representatives of the U.S. government. The representatives tried to persuade the islanders to join with Panama on their separation from Colombia. When the Nashville was approaching San Andres two teenage young men, John Suarez and Joab Escalona, rode their horses around the island, each one going in a different direction, announcing that this was possibly an enemy ship and they needed to be careful. The native islanders refused to join in seceding from

Colombia remembering their unhappy experiences which they had earlier when trying to study in a segregated system when they were refused entrance to most universities in the United States because of color.

The Panama Canal was inaugurated August 15, 1914, with the passing of the ship Ancon. Finally on March 24, 1928, Colombia, regrettably, with just a stroke of the pen, gave away the lands in which island natives and their Central American coastal families had lived and even some defended with their blood. Colombia and Nicaragua signed the treaty Esguerra-Barcenas, with the U.S. arbitrating. In this treaty, the republic of Colombia recognized the sovereignty and dominion of the republic of Nicaragua over the Miskito Coast from Cape Gracias a Dios to the San Juan River and over the Corn Islands in the Atlantic Ocean. In return, the republic of Nicaragua recognized the sovereignty and dominion of Colombia over the islands of San Andres and Providencia. The Keys of Roncador, Quita Sueño, and Serrana are not included in this treaty because these were in dispute between Colombia and the United States of America at the time of the treaty.

Chapter 4—Seventh day Adventism

Seventh day Adventists

The Seventh day Adventist Christian religion was introduced into the islands of San Andres and Providencia by Frank J. Huchins in 1900. Frank Huchins was born in 1869. Frank Huchins was originally from northern California. As a young man he worked as a stevedore in the San Francisco Bay area. He went to college at Healdsburg College in northern California and then to Battle Creek College in Michigan. He was offered ministerial work by the Seventh day Adventist church after graduation in 1891 but he declined because his dream was to become a medical missionary. He started to study medicine at the University of Michigan but after a few weeks he accepted an appointment to the Bay Islands of Honduras, Central America.

Pastor Huchins pioneered the Seventh day Adventist religion in the Bay Islands. While working there he realized the need for having adequate transportation between the islands and the mainland. He got the idea that he needed a boat similar to the Pitcairn. The Pitcairn was a schooner later rigged as a brigantine of 120 tons and used by the Seventh day Adventist missionaries in the South Pacific for ten years, 1890 to 1900. The General Conference of Seventh day Adventists voted to have a schooner built for missionary use in Central America so one was built by the Seventh day Adventist church members in the Bay Islands. This vessel was of 35 tons weight. Huchins became an excellent navigator and got the nick name 'Captain Storm' because of his many stormy adventures in the Caribbean Sea. This vessel was named the Herald. The Herald opened the way for Pastor Huchins to travel the Central American coast as well as the adjacent islands.

On one of these trips in late 1899 (during hurricane season) the Herald was surprised by a hurricane. Captain Storm tried to pass south of San Andres but was unable to do so. The hurricane winds were too strong and were increasing so Captain Storm (Pastor Huchins) decided to find safety in the island of San Andres. A sea captain on the island, Theodore Robinson, better known as Captain Tim, invited Elder Huchins to wait out the storm at his home. Elder Huchins shared the gospel with Captain Tim and his family and sold him some religious books before leaving.

Photo of Captain Theodore "Tim" Robinson

When Elder Huchins returned in early 1900 he found Captain Tim's family along with some other people keeping the seventh day Sabbath as the Bible commanded and wanting to be baptized. Elder Huchins preached the gospel to the interested ones and baptized eight persons.

An important member of Elder Huchins missionary team was Dr. John Eccles. Dr. Eccles settled on San Andres in March 1900. Later that year the missionary team formed by Elder Huchins, Dr. Eccles, and colporteurs, J.B. Haughton, Mr. Mateland, and Frank Mosebar went on the Herald to Providencia. They anchored in Old Town and from the deck of the schooner they attended to the dental and medical needs by day. At night, Elder Huchins preached on the following topics: the second coming of Jesus, His love, salvation from sins, the Judgment, and the end of the world. They also sold religious books. The first baptisms were Lawrence Robinson, Charlotte Hawkins Robinson, her daughters Muriel and Julia, Eunice Robinson (my grandmother), and her daughters Lissette and Estelle. These were the first Seventh day Adventist converts in Providencia. The first Adventists on the continent were not converted until twenty years later.

Captain Tim requested a teacher who would give his children a Christian education based on Seventh day Adventist

48

Christian principles. At his own expense Captain Tim provided not only the school house but a home and a salary for the teacher for many years. The Seventh day Adventist mission board responded in a most excellent manner, sending the best man they could find for the job. Samuel Parker Smith was chosen to go to the islands as the teacher. Samuel Parker Smith came from one of the families of the pioneers of the Seventh day Adventist church. His father was Uriah Smith, author of the outstanding book Daniel and Revelation. Uriah Smith was also editor of the *Review and Herald*, the official periodical of the Seventh day Adventist Church. He also held the position of Secretary Treasurer of the General Conference of Seventh day Adventists. The teacher sent to San Andres could not have had a better background and the product of his school proved him to be an excellent teacher.

In 1902, Dr. Eccles got sick with septicemia and died at the United Fruit Company Hospital in Bocas del Toro, Panama. Not long after this Elder Frank Huchins, while in Panama, came down with yellow fever and died on August 4, 1902, again in Bocas del Toro. Dr. Eccles and Elder Huchins are buried side by side. Shortly before Elder Huchins death the first Seventh day Adventist church in all of Colombia was organized in San Luis on the island of San Andres. Frank Huchins was a skillful navigator, dentist, piano tuner, but most of all an outstanding missionary preacher. He started the Adventist church in the archipelago of San Andres and Providencia and left it to be continued by others.

In the meantime, Mr. Parker Smith continued with the school and also directed the church work. Parker Smith was an outstanding teacher. He advised many of the parents to send their children to continue their education after completing their primary education in his school. He advised them to go to Jamaica or to the United States.

Zelotes Pusey was the first young man from Parker Smith's school to continue his studies in the United States of America. Captain Tim sent several of his children first to Jamaica then to the United States of America. Rudolph Newball was encouraged to go to the United States of America to study and he left in 1912. After working as a teacher and preacher for several years Parker Smith left the islands but the fruits of his work continued for many more years.

Zelotes Pusey had been instructed in Parker Smith's school then went to the United States where he studied medicine and dentistry. He returned to the island in 1912 being the first medical doctor that was a native of San Andres.

He graduated from Meharry Medical College in Tennessee and passed the state board examination. In addition he had the degree of DDS. He made a name for himself as a professional doctor and dentist.

Dr. Zelotes Pusey   **Florence Robinson**

Dr. Pusey had developed a friendship with Captain Tim's daughter Florence. When Florence returned from the United States her friendship with Dr. Pusey continued. Florence's family did not agree with the relationship between the two young people. Florence's grandmother, Mariah Williams, especially showed her displeasure because Dr. Pusey was very dark complexioned. It was rumored that Florence's family commented that Florence should never marry a black dog. The Robinsons were more interested in having Florence marry lawyer Dr. Francisco Newball, a good friend of the family. Dr. Newball was also the first native Intendente.

Dr. Pusey felt rejected and humiliated. Dr. Pusey wanted to marry Florence but she refused, not wanting to go against her family's wishes. One day some of Florence's friends wanted to go horseback riding and they invited Florence and her sisters, Neva and Ianthe. Florence did not want to go. Dr. Pusey sent her a note prohibiting her from going. Florence's grandmother, Mariah Williams, decided that Florence was going and sent her a horse. Dr. Pusey went to the place he knew they would pass. He took his revolver and waited where the horseback riders would be passing. Before getting to the spot in front of a guava orchard, Florence stopped at Leflet Kemble's house and asked for a drink of water. Mr. Kemble's daughter, Crisilda, my mother, brought Florence the glass of water. After drinking the water Florence and the riders continued. They passed by the guava plantation. Dr. Pusey came out of the guava orchard, grabbed the reins of Florence's horse, and asked her, 'Will you marry me?' She answered 'No, I can't.' He answered, 'If you can't be mine, you can't be for anyone else.' Right there and then, to the astonishment of her sisters and friends, he shot Florence and laid her on the ground, dead. One of the riders rushed to tell Captain Tim that Dr. Pusey had killed Florence. Captain Tim hurried to the place. Dr. Pusey shot Captain Tim when he arrived. Captain Tim died instantly. Captain Tim's eldest son, Fredrick, was working nearby, heard the shots, and came out to investigate. When Fredrick learned what had happened he ran toward Dr. Pusey, machete in hand. Dr. Pusey started running and tried to shoot at Fredrick but stumbled and shot himself. When Fredrick saw Dr. Pusey he raised his machete to kill him but Dr. Pusey pleaded for his life. Some of the neighbors also told Fredrick not to stain his hands with a man's blood so he did not use his machete. He later said that not finishing off Dr. Pusey was the best decision of his whole life. Dr. Pusey died of his self-inflicted wound March 23, 1915. This was indeed one of the saddest days to be remembered in San Andres. Two young and promising lives and that of a great community and church leader had ended in tragedy. Some non-Adventists called the Adventist church "the church of bandits." After this tragedy for some time there was no minister to lead the Seventh day Adventist church but the members continued with only an occasional visit from ministers from the Panama Conference.

Captain Sherry

Captain Sheridan Archbold was an excellent seaman. Several future captains studied navigation under him. Captain Sherry, as he was called, was captain of the schooner Excelsior. On a certain trip he was guiding his ship from San Andres to Providencia. The vessel was empty. A squall came up and before the sails could be lowered the schooner capsized and sank. Most of the crew, in two small boats, were able to reach Puerto Limon, Costa Rica. After this no one would employ Captain Sherry as a captain.

**Photo of Charlotte Hawkins and Uncle Percy
Robinson**

Captain Sherry's mother-in-law, Charlotte Hawkins
Robinson, and some of her daughters were in the first group of
people to be baptized into the Seventh day Adventist church
on Providencia. Charlotte Hawkins Robinson loved to share
her faith. When she was baptized into the Seventh day
Adventist church, as stated previously, she was part of the
group that were the first converts. She taught her new found
faith to her daughter, Matilda and her son-in-law, Sheridan
Archbold. They were both baptized and joined the Seventh
day Adventist church in 1905 by Pastor I.J. Knight. Captain
Sherry became the leader of the Seventh day Adventist church
in Saint Isabel, Providencia and served until his death on
December 26, 1976, at the age of 97. His wife lived to be
almost 100 years old, from August 31, 1881, to April 25, 1981.

Charlotte's husband, Percival Robinson was a sailor.
When he returned home from one of his trips he found out that
his wife had become a Seventh day Adventist. He was so
enraged that he packed up his clothes and went back to sea.
His wife placed some religious tracks among his clothes,
unknown to him. He was gone for about two months but
when he returned he requested baptism into the Seventh day
Adventist church. Uncle Percy, as he was known, became a

pillar in the Seventh day Adventist church in Saint Isabel, Providencia.

As Uncle Percy grew older he developed dizziness whenever he closed his eyes so that whenever he prayed he did so with his eyes open. One Sabbath just before the sermon by Captain Sherry, Uncle Percy was asked to give the main prayer. Uncle Percy, with his eyes wide open, started to pray. The cow pasture near the church was owned by Uncle Percy's daughter, Muriel. Evidently the grass was not mature enough for the cows to eat. Suddenly Uncle Percy interrupted his prayer with a shout to his grandson Lisandro, 'Sandy! Sandy! Go chase the cows out of the grass piece!' Then he continued his prayer as if nothing had happened.

After the terrible hurricane of 1940, where most of the houses on Providencia, including the Seventh day Adventist church, were destroyed, church services were held in Captain Sherry's house. Once more Uncle Percy was asked to pray so, with his eyes wide open, he started his prayer. After praying for a few seconds he blurted out, 'Brother Sherry! Brother Sherry! The chickens are in the watermelon patch eating the watermelons!' Captain Sherry answered, 'Never mind, just pray.' The young people present could not help but snicker.

Joe Gomez

Joe Gomez was a Miskito Indian. He was a member of the Seventh day Adventist church in San Luis, San Andres. Brother Joe, as he was called, never preached. Brother Joe never taught a Sabbath school lesson. Brother Joe never gave Bible studies. He would open the church for Sabbath services and he would open or close the windows as needed. Brother Joe owned a coconut plantation. When the disease destroyed the coconut palms on San Andres, brother Joe made the decision that no matter what he would continue to pay a faithful tithe. Not a single coconut palm of brother Joe's developed the disease and his respect in the community was increased 100%.

Jane Duffis lived in San Andres. Her daughter was living in Curacao. Jane went to visit her daughter when her daughter was giving birth to her first child. Her daughter had become a Seventh day Adventist and Jane questioned her about her strange beliefs. Jane returned to San Andres where she was a Sunday school teacher in the Baptist church. The topic of her class on the first Sunday was on the ten commandments. She prepared her lesson but had questions in her mind and so went to visit her pastor. She asked him why it was that her Bible says to keep the seventh day Sabbath but yet they were worshiping on Sunday. The pastor told her that the Bible Sabbath had never been changed but that we keep Sunday to celebrate the resurrection of Jesus. When she stood up before her class she stated, 'This will be my last day as a teacher because I cannot reconcile what the Bible says with what I am doing. From now on I will be going to the Seventh day Adventist church.' When her husband, Alfred Duffis, heard that she was going to the Seventh day Adventist church he was furious and he told her, 'The only way you can go to the Adventist church is over my dead body.' Two weeks later Alfred Duffis died and a month later Jane joined the Seventh day Adventist church on profession of faith.

When the slaves were freed many of them were given some property by their masters and these ex-slaves cultivated their land and even were able to employ other former slaves. These ex-slaves and descendants of slaves preferred to work for black property owners than for their previous white masters. In the course of time some of these black property owners became wealthy. Among these black property owners was Nafthali Pomaire. Over the years he saved his money and became wealthy. Then Mr. Pomaire, when he got old, wanted to keep his money safe so he decided to find an honest carpenter who could also keep a secret. He decided that the most honest carpenter on San Andres was Fred Osmond, a member of the Seventh day Adventist church. Mr. Osmond built a secret compartment in Mr. Pomaire's house and kept the secret of where the money was. After Mr. Pomaire's death unfortunately the money was stolen but the thief was never found.

Rudolph Newball

Rudolph T. Newball was born in Providencia November 16, 1882. As a young man he was a seaman and became an excellent navigator. He traveled to Cuba and to the Colombian coast of Central America (now Panama). In Panama he found some very fertile land and decided to plant coconuts. He also built a camp house on the property near the beach.

One day Rudolph was working by himself until after dark. He decided to go back to camp, walking on the beach. In the dark he saw what looked like a log in the water. What was a little strange was that the log was moving in the same direction and at the same speed as Rudolph was. He stopped to closer investigate and was greeted by two large, shining eyes and he realized that it was not a log but a large snake. He decided to use his sharp machete to sink it into the snake just behind his head. To his amazement he was successful. He looked to see if the snake would follow him but it did not. He went to camp then the next morning while walking on the beach he saw the huge snake lying on the ground, dead. After examining the wound that he had inflicted to the snake even though he was not a church going man he decided that some divine power had helped him do such a job.

A few days later just after dark Rudolph saw something coming toward him. He went with his machete to investigate and realized that it was a man with a box of books on his shoulder. He told the man that it was dangerous to walk on the beach at night then helped him with the box full of books. The man was a member of the crew from the schooner Herald with religious books for sale. He sold Rudolph some books and told him to keep in good health, indicating the ill effects of tobacco. One evening after the man from the Herald had left, Rudolph was returning to camp and felt the need of a chew. He reached in his bag for a piece of tobacco. He thought he heard the voice of the man from the Herald saying, 'Your body is temple of the living God.' He saw no one but took his bag of tobacco, tied a stone to it, and threw it as far as he could into the sea. He never used tobacco in any form since.

After this, Rudolph went to Bocas del Toro where he joined the Seventh day Adventist church. After becoming an Adventist, Rudolph promised God that if he gave him an Adventist wife and enough money he would go to an Adventist university in the United States and that he would work for Him the rest of his life. He returned to Providencia and there married Elma, the daughter of Pastor McLaughlin, a Presbyterian minister. Elma was an Adventist. He married Elma after two weeks of courtship. Soon after this, he received a letter from the Baker Company of White Plains, New York, wanting to buy his coconut plantation. He met with them and they bought his land for much more than he was going to ask.

The promise that Rudolph had made to God that if he could have an Adventist wife and enough money he would study to prepare to serve the Lord and work for Him for the rest of his life kept gnawing at his mind. In the meantime Parker Smith and Rudolph became friends. Parker Smith supplied Rudolph with books to stimulate his mind and encouraged him to go to the United States to study. So in

1912 Rudolph Newball was accepted by Oakwood College of Huntsville, Alabama where he studied theology. But he wanted to be a teacher. He also learned the art of broom making. This served him well for the rest of his life to supplement his income.

Rudolph Newball returned to Providencia after graduation and founded the Rocky Point School which, for many years, was the most outstanding school of the archipelago. Many of the students that went to this school became famous men and women, not only in the islands of San Andres and Providencia but in Colombia, the Caribbean, Central America, as well as the United States of America. Many of the students from Rocky Point continued their studies in Las Cascadas, Panama. Rudolph Newball was a professor between 1926 and 1930 at this school. He also was a professor at Instituto Colombo Venezolano in Medellin Colombia in the 1940s. However for most of his life Rudolph T. Newball was the leader of the Seventh day Adventist church in San Andres and Providencia. He died in Providencia on January 9, 1978.

Bender Archbold

Probably the most outstanding missionary from the islands of San Andres and Providencia, and one of the most famous Seventh day Adventist ministers in the whole world, was Bender Lawton Archbold. Bender Archbold was the son of Captain Sheridan Archbold and his wife Matilda. Bender was born August 12, 1908, in Providencia. He studied at Rocky Point School under Rudolph Newball then at West Caribbean Training School in Las Cascadas, Panama. He studied business administration at La Sierra College in California and religion, English, and business at Pacific Union College, also in California. He received a Masters Degree in school administration and education psychology at Andrews University in Michigan.

Bender was chairman of the English department at West Indies College in Jamaica. He was the first person not to be born in the United States to occupy the following positions: principal of Panamanian Industrial College, departmental secretary of Caribbean Union for youth and education, president of the South Caribbean Conference of Seventh Day Adventists 1951-1957, president of Caribbean Union College 1957-1962. He was moved up to the Inter-American Division of Seventh day Adventists as secretary of lay activities 1962-1966, then secretary of the division from 1966-1970, then the first Latin American to become president of the Inter-

American Division of Seventh day Adventists and vice
president of the General Conference of the Seventh day
Adventist worldwide church from 1970-1980. He was then
requested to be the president of the General Conference of the
worldwide church of Seventh day Adventists but he declined.
Under his administration at the Inter-American division it
grew to become the largest division of the Seventh day
Adventist worldwide church. Elder Bender Archbold has
never forgotten his roots and has visited his islands many
times. He has promoted the advancement of his island home
from his office in the United States. He died when he was
almost 100 years old.

Photo of Bender Archbold

Bender was honored with a place in the alumni hall of
fame in 1974 and was granted an honorary doctors degree in
divinity in 1979 from Andrews University. He was the first
pastor to receive such an honor.

There have been many leaders of the Seventh day
Adventist church who came from San Andres and Providencia.
In fact, the percentage of missionaries, relative to the

population is greater from Providencia than from any other part of the world. We will mention a few of these leaders without elaboration: Sheridan Archbold and his sons Wilton, Bender and Fulton, Rudolph Newball, Ricardo Rankin, Mario Robinson, Augusto Britton, Wing Chi Chow, Daniel Duffis, Earl Newball. Jeddy Hooker, Carlos A. Archbold and Felix Archbold.

Photo of Ricardo Rankin, Rudolph Newball, Sheridan Archbold and Bender Archbold

The Klondike and the 1932 Hurricane

The Klondike was a schooner of 65 tons owned by four men from the Robinson family. The Klondike was anchored in Smooth Water Bay Harbor because the captain's home was there. On November 5, 1932, the wind started to blow. The captain put out the two anchors that were available then went home, leaving the Klondike in the care of two of his trusted sailors.

This hurricane left the island of Providencia in ruins. Thirty-five houses fell. All the coconut, orange, and other fruit trees were destroyed. In the night of November 5 the violence of the storm increased. The chain to the larger of the two anchors on the Klondike snapped. The vessel started to drag the smaller anchor.

Earlier in the evening two of the owners of the Klondike were at Bible study. One of the men present lead in prayer and asked God that if it was not God's will to check the storm that He would somehow save the Klondike. The vessel continued to drag the small anchor. All human hope for the rescue of the Klondike was gone. Lorenzo Robinson one of the two men on board, told me that the dragging suddenly stopped in spite of the increasing violence of the storm. When the hurricane had passed the Klondike had not moved any more and was safe. Captain Lorenzo stated that the anchor that was being dragged by the Klondike got caught between two rocks in the bottom of the sea and held fast. With the violence of the storm the chain that held this anchor through the night bored through the metal protection and even started to break through the hull of the vessel but when the storm subsided the Klondike was miraculously safe. Was this due to two rocks in the bottom of the sea or was it an answer to prayer?

Chapter 5—Early Twentieth Century

Around the end of the nineteenth century and the first part of the twentieth century several Europeans settled in the islands of San Andres and Providencia. Two of them were very controversial and interesting.

Herman Von Tietje
The first was Herman Von Tietje, at times called Von Tickenback. Tietje is an abbreviation of sorts of Tickenback. Some people say Von Tietje arrived in Providencia in 1910, others 1914. He made two interesting claims. First he claimed to be involved in the Mayrling incident in Austria where the crown prince of the Hapsburg empire of Austria Hungary was found dead of a self inflicted gunshot wound to the head lying next to his lover, Baroness Vetrera. Countess Lariesch had acted as go between for the two lovers. After this suicide and murder she divorced her husband, Count George Lariesch. There is a remote possibility that Von Tietje was really Count George Lariesch who had been banished from the royal household with his wife. Second, although he showed no evidence of medical training he practiced medicine for more than 21 years in Providencia until his death in 1931. He delivered babies and trained midwives including Mariana Archbold, who delivered my younger brother, Efren. Dr. Tietje claimed to be a specialist in curing hemorrhoids and all the diseases of the male and female sexual organs as well as problems of the nose, throat, and lungs. He claimed that his treatment for malaria never failed.

When Von Tietje was on his death bed in 1931 he asked Captain Ephriem Archbold to place a notice in the newspaper Star and Herald of Panama stating that Herman Von Tikenback had died.

Karl Bernhard Regnier
The second controversial person from Europe to settle in the islands was Karl Bernhard Regnier who came with two other Germans in 1935. Regnier and his companions lived on the top of High Peak, the highest point on the island of Providencia. Regnier had been a German fighter pilot during World War I and had earned the iron cross for his valor. These Germans built a powerful search light on the peak with which he allegedly signaled German submarines. Regnier married

Rachel Rankin, sister of James Rankin, Jr. Regnier walked with a limp, the result of a World War I injury.

Regnier established a general store in San Andres on the waterfront in North End. Soon he became the most successful merchant in San Andres. He undersold all the other merchants. For example, it was said that the other merchants sold flour for 7 cents a pound whereas Regnier was selling it for 5 cents a pound. Regnier also had a wharf that was joined to his store and which facilitated the transport of merchandise. Many people believe that German submarines frequently came into the cove on the western side of San Andres. The road to the cove was in a poor state of repair but even so Regnier's truck, driven by Owen Kelly, traveled over that road twice per week. Regnier's brother in law, James Rankin, was pro-Nazi. Many people think that Regnier was a German spy and that he and Rankin supplied fuel to the German submarines.

Before World War II, Colombia and Germany had very good relations. Trade between the two countries was brisk. Many German companies had offices and business in Colombia. There were German technicians and instructors in the Colombian navy as well. There are rumors that during the war Germany invited Colombia to enter the war on the side of the axis powers and that Germany would return Panama and the canal to Colombia when Germany would be victorious.

World War II had a tremendous influence on the islands of San Andres and Providencia. At first the islands were positively influenced because the islanders found ready employment in the Canal Zone but later there was a severely negative impact. Let's continue with the history which, in part, is controversial. As part of the German war effort U-boats were sent to the Caribbean to interrupt the U.S. activity to and from the Panama Canal Zone as well as sinking oil tankers transporting petroleum to the United States to supply the allied war effort.

German submarines stationed in Europe, in order to cross the Atlantic ocean and be active against the allies in the Caribbean would require refueling somewhere before returning to home base in Europe. Therefore it was suggested that there was an extensive supply network for the fueling of German submarines. One of the U.S. Navy's most exasperating tasks was the investigation of rumors that enemy submarines were using Central America for refueling. There were many stories of schooners taking diesel oil in drums to U-boats. Schooners from San Andres were said to be included in this extensive supply network. This was never proven, however there were some facts that were circumstantial evidence.

The Blue Stream

Two United States citizens, Hemingway and Jenkinson, were convinced of the pro German supply network and they were eager to prove it. As to which Hemingway was involved, there is a controversy. Most historians are convinced that this was Leicester Hemingway, a newspaper man from San Francisco and brother of Earnest Hemingway. The article in the San Francisco Chronicle and the one in the Reader's Digest about this trip to Central America and to the Western Caribbean both were signed by Leicester Hemingway. On the other hand, the natives of Providencia believe that this was no other than Earnest Hemingway himself who, in these articles, used a pseudonym so as not to be bothered by the U.S. investigators while he was working on the novel The Old Man and the Sea.

I was in Providencia while these men visited. I was a boy of 13 years of age at the time. I was introduced by my father Walter Robinson to a man as the great writer Earnest Hemingway. This man shook my hand without acknowledging or denying this statement.

Hemingway and Jenkinson, on their small schooner the Blue Stream, sailed from Key West down the Central American coast to Panama and visited San Andres and Providencia. In the Bay Islands as well as the Central American countries the two investigators were sure that they had proof of the supply network. In San Andres they saw Bernhard Regnier's waterfront store as well as his wharf. They then proceeded to Providencia. While there James Rankin's schooner of 52 tons, the Resolute, came into port. The captain of the Resolute was Captain Eliseo Hawkins. Hemingway met Captain Hawkins who was loading some diesel drums onto the Resolute. Hemingway said, "Captain Hawkins, what do you have in these drums?" He answered, "Water." "What does water from diesel drums taste like?" was the next question. "Just like mother's milk," came the captain's answer.

About two nights later around 8:30 Hemingway went to James Rankin's general store. My father, Walter Robinson, was the manager of the store. "Please sell me ten pounds of cheese." Hemingway requested. "The store is now closed but I will sell you the cheese," was the answer. Hemingway then paid for the cheese with a $100 bill. Walter Robinson, who had not seen a $100 bill for a long time said, "I have already turned the cash in to James Rankin. Come back in the morning and pay me." In the morning there was no Blue Stream in sight so, to this day, it is a family joke that Hemingway owes my father for 10 pounds of cheese.

The rumors continued that several islanders were selling diesel fuel to the Germans and among the suspects were Bernhard Regnier, James Rankin, Roosevelt Robinson, and several others. As soon as Hemingway's article was published, Captain Eliseo Hawkins got off the Resolute, went to his home in Lazy Hill, and never went back to sea until after the war was over. Captain Baldwin Britton related to his sons how he would rendezvous with the German submarines on the Keys of Serrana and Roncador. Captain Roosevelt Robinson, part owner and captain of the schooner Ziroma, was chased by the Colombian navy. One of the naval ships chasing the Ziroma was under the command of Captain Franco Robinson, Roosevelt's brother. The Ziroma was never captured. Roosevelt was suspicious of the efforts to capture him so he asked Captain Orville Archbold to take command of the Ziroma. The Ziroma, under the command of Orville Archbold was stopped by a submarine. The captain of the submarine demanded to see the captain. He asked the captain what was his name. He responded "Orville Archbold" and convinced the submarine officer that Roosevelt was not on board. The sub then let the Ziroma go. Maxwell Newball, owner and captain of the schooner Gloria was also stopped by a submarine. Some of the crew from the submarine boarded the Gloria. They took the short wave radio and scolded the captain but did not find who they were looking for.

Photo of a Two-Masted Schooner Rigged Like the Ziroma

Vessels Sunk in World War II

The war touched the people of the islands of Sand Andres and Providencia when four of the vessels were sunk: the Resolute, the Ruby, the Roamer and the Envoy.

I want to clarify first that the schooner Tres Amigos was not sunk by anyone. Sometime before the others were gunned down the Tres Amigos, under captain Elkanah Archbold, with very little cargo on board was hit by a squall and capsized. Some of the crew accused captain Elkanah of having the vessel under too much canvas. However, captain Elkanah related to my father in my presence that he was in the process of taking a time sight of the sun to find his longitude when a squall hit and turned the schooner over without giving any time to adjust the sails.

The tragedies of World War II did not leave the islands of Providencia and San Andres untouched. Many American ships traveling to and from the Panama Canal Zone and oil tankers transporting oil from Venezuela and Colombia were sunk by the German U-boats. The island vessels picked up and saved many shipwrecked American sailors. My father saved the crew of oil tankers more than once and took them to Colon when he was captain of the schooner Hilda.

Photo of a Two-Masted Schooner Rigged Like the Resolute

The Resolute was a sailing schooner of 52 tons. She was owned by James Rankin Jr., traveled between San Andres, Providencia, Cartagena, and Colon. She carried coconuts and copra (dried coconuts) from the islands and brought merchandise to the islands for James Rankin, Bernhard Regnier, and others. Early in June 1942 the Resolute left Providencia for Cartagena. Her captain was Alvan Mc Lean. On the way to Cartagena the crew of the Resolute picked up 28 survivors from a ship and took them safely to Cartagena. On the way back, on the morning of June 23 when the Resolute was 35 miles from San Andres a submarine surfaced and started shooting without warning.

Let's pick up the story as told by Captain McLean: 'I was in command of the vessel Resolute with seven people on board. Without warning a periscope appeared and a submarine surfaced. Four soldiers with gas masks started to shoot at us. I gave orders to Hiron Archbold to hoist the Colombian flag just in case there had been a mistake of identity. Hiron had just hoisted the flag when a second flurry of shots left Hiron Archbold dead beneath the flag. I then ordered Ignacio Barker to adjust the jibs so that we could stop the vessel but a shower of bullets left him dead on the bow of the vessel. I saw that a bullet took off one finger of Misael Santana and, at that instant; I was hit once in the left forearm and once in the shoulder. In a desperate effort to save our lives we were able to get into a small boat which was full of bullet holes. Doris (Fox), without consulting anyone, tore her dress and with the pieces sealed the holes in the boat one by one. In this way she saved us from sure death.'

Doris was the heroine of this terrible situation. She was an excellent swimmer and saved the wounded one by one by swimming to them, taking them to the boat, and helping them into the boat. Then, once in the boat, she stopped all the bullet holes with her own clothes so that the boat would not sink and the survivors were able to get to land.

The survivors were Captain Alvan McLean, a sailor named James Newball who was a very short man and two passengers, Misael Santana, who was wounded, and Doris Fox, the heroine. All the others were lost.

The Resolute was finished off with hand grenades thrown from the submarine. An American hydroplane was sent from the Canal Zone to take the wounded to Panama and the Intendente gave permission. However, James Rankin, the owner of the Resolute, thinking that perhaps someone would say something against him, only let Captain Mc Lean and

Misael Santana go. Captain McLean stated that the
Colombian government had sent $800 to be divided among the
victims but the counsel only gave $40. Doris Fox was so
traumatized psychologically that she refused to discuss this
incident forever thereafter.

The saga of the sinking of the Resolute was put into song
with a very catchy tune so that even today it is a favorite of all
island dance halls. Some of the stanzas, as I remember them,
are stated here. There is a stanza for each person involved.
This song is written in archaic island English where the past
tense is only occasionally used.

Alvan fly to Colon in American aeroplane (repeat four
times)

Manoah was the one who eat the German ball
Manoah was the one who eat the German ball
Manoah was the one who eat the German ball
Alvan fly to Colon in American aeroplane

Doris was the swimmer who swim to save the rest
Doris was the swimmer who swim to save the rest
Doris was the swimmer who swim to save the rest
Alvan fly to Colon in American aeroplane

Jamesy was so small he hid behind the mast
Jamesy was so small he hid behind the mast
Jamesy was so small he never get a ball
Alvan fly to Colon in American aeroplane

When James Rankin hear the plane he tremble like a leaf
When James Rankin hear the plane he tremble like a leaf
When James Rankin hear the plane he tremble like a leaf
Alvan fly to Colon in American aeroplane

The next schooner to be a casualty of the war was the
Ruby. The Ruby was 38 tons in size (approximately the same
size as the Herald, mentioned above). The owner of the Ruby
was Captain Elkhenah Archbold. The usual captain was
Captain Nicholas Newball, better known as Captain Chung.
On her last voyage, Captain Elkhenah took command of the
Ruby and Captain Chung stayed at home. The vessel was
attacked by a submarine and miserably destroyed and sunk.
With the first burst of gunfire Captain Elkhenah came out of
his cabin and pleaded for mercy but the answer was a bullet to

his neck killing him instantly. Some of the crew were killed but there were some survivors who reached Colon.

Some of the survivors of the Ruby related that English was spoken on the submarine and also that the identifying numbers on the submarine were identical to those on a sub in Cristobal, Panama.

Photo of a Three-Masted Schooner Rigged Like the Roamar

The next tragedy was that of the Roamar. Previously its name was Urios. The Roamar was a three masted schooner, registered as 110 tons. Part owner and Captain was Samuel May. Captain Sam May had served the Colombian navy as instructor of navigation and as a captain of the naval ship Cabimas. Captain Sam May also played a vital part in the war between Colombia and Peru in the 1930s.

Captain May was on a voyage between San Andres and Cartagena. The Roamar was stopped by a submarine. The captain of the submarine knew Captain May and greeted him cordially, reminding him of the days when both of them were instructors in the Colombian navy. The submarine captain said to Captain Sam May, 'Captain May, you're an old man. Go home and do not go back to the sea any more. I have orders to sink this ship.' It must be stated that there were American, British, and German instructors in the Colombian navy. When Captain May returned to San Andres the Roamar laid at anchor for quite some time. After three weeks Captain May became restless. As far as is known, Captain May did not reveal the nationality of the captain of the submarine that had stopped him and given him the warning even though the consensus is that the language used was probably English.

After a few soul searching days Captain May and his crew, including his own son Hadley, sailed for Cartagena, arriving there safely and without incident. After loading needed supplies and taking on many passengers, including members of the families of army captain Castro and Milciades Martinez, the Roamar left for San Andres. Almost arriving to San Andres they were in the area of East South East Key when the Roamar was sunk. There were no survivors. In fact, some people on San Andres say they heard the explosion.

It is not known who sank the Resolute, the Ruby, or the Roamar. There are two theories which will be discussed shortly.

The Envoy was a 30 ton sloop partially owned by Leon Wilson and Captain Wellington Hooker, better known as Fenton Hooker. There are various theories as to where she was going on her last trip. The truth will be told here. My father, Walter Robinson, had a business in Cartagena where he dried coconuts making copra. Copra is used in making vegetable shortening and soap. Walter Robinson got his supply of coconuts from San Andres. Because of what we just related the insurance on the transport of coconuts was very high, making Walter Robinson's profit very small. Mr. Walter decided that he would not insure just one cargo of coconuts. So the Envoy left San Andres with 40,000 coconuts, uninsured. World War II was still going on. Even though the danger from German submarines had lessened ships still traveled without running lights at night. The Envoy, without lights, saw a destroyer approaching and, according to the crew, tried to avoid a collision by tacking. However the destroyer hit the Envoy from behind and the Envoy was split wide open and sank. No lives were lost.

The Americans acknowledge that it was an American ship that collided with the Envoy accidentally. Captain Fenton Hooker and the crew of the Envoy think it was not an accident for the following reason: James Rankin was known to be pro-Nazi and, as stated above, he was accused of supplying fuel to the Germans. James Rankin was on the allied black list. James Rankin had secured passage on the Envoy to go from San Andres to Cartagena. At the last minute James Rankin canceled his trip. The crew of the Envoy and many others believe that the Americans were out to get James Rankin. One thing was for sure, that the sinking of the Envoy caused Walter Robinson to go bankrupt.

For the benefit of the reader who might not be familiar with sailing, the following needs to be made clear. When a motor vessel (steamship) is going from San Andres or Providence to Cartagena it may follow a direct southeast course to their destination. For a sailing vessel this might not always be possible. For most of the year the trade winds blow from the Southeast, so that a sailing vessel would find it impossible to travel directly into the wind. For this reason a sailing ship going from the Colombian Islands to Cartagena or Puerto Colombia will first go south towards the Panamanian Coast then go east crossing the Gulf of Darien (Uraba) and then to Cartagena. This explains why both the Ruby and the Envoy were nearer to Colon than to Cartagena when they were sunk.

Who sank the Resolute, Ruby, and Roamar, and why? On the one side there are those who say it was the Germans. They say that the suppliers of the fuel to the German submarines did not fulfill their side of the bargain. The historian J.C. Robinson says that there are official documents in which the Germans admit sinking these schooners and they gave dates and position of each sinking. He even gives the identity of each submarine. For the Resolute, U-172; for the Ruby, U-516; Roamar, commanded by Lieutenant Alex Olaf Loewe, U-505. The official position of Colombia is that the Germans did it.

On the other side many say that it is not logical for the Germans to destroy the very ones who were helping them by providing fuel and food but that it was the Americans who were only trying to defeat the Germans by cutting off their fuel supply. Some of the survivors of the Ruby said that English was the language that they heard coming from the submarine and some said that the identifying numbers on the submarine were identical with the numbers on an American submarine that they saw in the Canal Zone.

There was a young woman from Bottom House who worked in the home of an American naval officer on the Canal Zone. Her bedroom was adjacent to the master bedroom. She said that one night when the naval officer came home that she heard him telling his wife that he was so sorry for what he had to do that day in sinking a vessel that had many pretty girls on board. This was at the same time that the Roamar was sunk.

Recently a friend of mine, Maxine Newball, told me that her Aunt Lola was married to an American navy man and that he told Lola that it was the Americans that sank the island schooners. It is up to you, reader, to make up your own mind as to who sank the Resolute, the Ruby, and the Roamar.

Islanders in the War with Peru

In the year 1932, Peru and Colombia were at war. Peru invaded Colombia's territory in the Amazon area. The Colombian navy had a few gun boats but no one to command them. San Andres and Providencia came to the rescue of the mother country with scores of volunteers consisting of sailors, engineers, and sea captains who were able to take command of the ships. The captains proceeded to take the ships up the Amazon River and defend the Colombian territory of its southern border, thereby Colombia was victorious. This was due in no small part to the efforts of the navy consisting, in its majority, of islanders. Some of the islanders were: Captain Samuel May, Captain John Suarez, Captain Enrique Palacio, Captain Alston Newball, Marvin Tayler, Manuel Robinson, Woodrow Robinson, and many others who helped to return Colombian sovereignty to the area around Leticia. Colombia did not officially recognize the islands' contribution in their victory over Peru until very recently and by this time most of the islanders that took part were already dead.

Chapter 6—Sports and Culture

Sports

Another contribution of the islanders to the welfare of Colombia was in the area of sports. In general, the natives of the islands of San Andres and Providencia are bigger and taller than the Colombians from the continent and have considerable athletic ability. Baseball was first played in San Andres before it was played on the continent where football (soccer) was the main sport. Baseball was brought to San Andres from Nicaragua, Panama and from the United States by students who were returning home. It was first promoted by John Myers. He did not find it too difficult to introduce this new game because the game that was played before on the islands was cricket. Three teams were formed: the Pink Boys, later changed their name to the Red Lyons, were from the hill; the Blue Boys from North End and the Hot Stuff from the southern part of the island, most of them from San Luis and Sound Bay. Students from the islands introduced baseball to the rest of Colombia, first to Cartagena and Barranquilla, then later to Bogota, Medellin, and Barranca Bermeja.

Many outstanding players represented the islands on the continent and even in the major leagues of the United States. Some of the outstanding island baseball players were: John Astor Cupidan, short stop and pitcher, known as 'Little John,' John Kellman, catcher, known as 'Big John.' These two played for the Red Lions. Zacheus Powell was a great pitcher of the Blue Boys in the early days. Manassah Stephens was a great hitter of the Hot Stuff. Another great player of the Hot Stuff, I do not know his name, but his nick name was 'Guana.' Horace Smith was a catcher and great home run hitter. Castelio Archbold was a great pitcher who, it is said, struck out the great short stop and hitter of Cartagena, Chita Miranda three times in one game. Jaime Velez was another great player. Enrique Suarez was an outstanding pitcher. Wellingworth May was an outstanding short stop, pitcher, and manager. Vedison Bernard, better known as 'Prophet,' pitched a no hit, no run game against Cartagena into the ninth inning, only to lose the game when an outfielder dropped the ball. Humberto Robinson pitched in the major leagues with the Milwaukee Braves and the Cincinnati Reds.

Edison Christopher was an outstanding first baseman known for his long home runs. He was also probably the best basketball player Colombia ever produced. When the basketball team the San Francisco Dons, with their great player Bill Russell, toured Colombia; Edison Christopher scored 27 points in a game against Bill Russell and company, his 27 points being more than half of the points of his team.

Culture
A few words need to be said about the basic culture of the islands of San Andres and Providencia. The way the people lived, as I know it, is the way they lived during the last half of the nineteenth century and the first half of the twentieth century. Starting in the last half of the twentieth century the culture of these islands has changed a lot even though some things remain the same.

I will talk about language the way I know and experienced it. English, Spanish, and Patois (Creole) are the languages. There have always been people who speak standard English. Most of the islanders speak an archaic English that the islanders themselves call Elizabethan English. A few examples of Elizabethan English are: fetch, instead of bring; bush, instead of forest or jungle; row, instead of argument or dispute; make baby, instead of to be pregnant; vex, instead of angry. Many speak broken English. Some people will go from standard English to Elizabethan English to broken English depending on the person they are speaking with. Spanish was spoken by a few at first but now everyone can speak Spanish.

Patois or Creole is understood by all and spoken by a majority of the islanders. Creole, according to anthropologist Dr. Jay Edwards of Michigan, is a language and not a dialect. It is a mixture of English, Spanish, Portuguese, French, and West African languages. It was first spoken by the slaves when they did not want their masters to understand what they were saying. In some respect it is more expressive than either English or Spanish. Examples: Juck iym, is more expressive than, cut him; Wi guaine nyam, is more expressive than, it is dinner time.

The last time I was in San Andres, I sat next to a young lady on a bus and started to speak to her in English. To my surprise, she answered in Spanish, "I don't speak English, only Spanish or Creole." I asked her if she was an islander. She answered yes but repeated that she only spoke Spanish or Creole. English is fast dying out on San Andres. Schools are all taught now in Spanish whereas some used to be taught in English and some in Spanish. Some church services are still performed in English, others in Spanish.

During the period when I lived on the islands there were many poor people but very few beggars and almost everyone had enough to eat. The general living conditions, as I recall, were similar to what is described by my friend and historian, Wall Petersen in his book The Province of Providence. On the islands it was very common to have a regular kitchen and then an additional one joined or separate. This additional kitchen was called 'greje.' In the additional one wood was used and this served to smoke meats, prepare fruit preserves, and to bake bread, cakes, and puddings. The meats and fish were salted and pickled, then hung up and smoked. Cakes and puddings were made from plantains, corn, cassava, sweet potatoes, cocos and other tuberous plants.

The whole community would take part in the processing of sugar cane, coconut oil, and cassava (known also as yucca, which is Spanish for cassava). The cane grind, the processing of sugar cane into sugar products, was a community affair. Sugar cane was extensively planted on both San Andres and on Providencia. The time to harvest sugar cane was the latter part of January into February and March. There were portable cane mills that were transported from one plantation to another during the grinding season, while each farmer took his turn. Volunteers would cut the cane, the mill would be set up, wood and coconut husks were brought to be used as fuel. The cane was brought to the mill. A man fed the cane into the mill, which was turned by two horses while a boy with a whip ran behind each horse. The delicious cane juice flowed into a drum. The man in charge of boiling would take the juice from the drum and pour it into the caldrons (called 'coppers'). The liquid would begin to boil. The boiler would use a long pole with a strainer to skim off the impurities, leaving the syrup free of impurities. The boiling was usually done at night because the boiling would be too hot during the day and the process was not finished until about 4 o'clock in the morning. The cane grind was a major social affair enjoyed by all. There was singing accompanied by guitar and accordion music. It was even a time for courting.

Another community endeavor was the harvesting and processing of cassava. The men would dig up the cassava then the women would peel and grate it. The grated material was then mixed with water and strained into a tub. The portion that settled in the bottom of the tub was starch that would be used later for starching clothes. This starch is also the source of tapioca, though tapioca is not produced on the island. The remainder of the plant material is dried then grated again,

73

forming flour. From the cassava various foods are made such as bammy, a flat bread similar to a tortilla, cassava cake (also called juck burro), a sweet pudding style cake, porridge, and dumpling.

Coconuts were the chief export from the islands. The best coconuts are called 'select' and this is what is exported. The culls and rejects were taken by the ladies of the community who would chip, grate, and strain the milk of these rejected coconuts, then boil and process the liquid until the water evaporated, leaving only clear, pure oil. This oil is used for cooking or sent to Colon and Cartagena to be sold. From coconuts the islanders make coconut cakes, which are ball shaped treats made of coconut mixed with cane syrup. There is a similar treat made with sesame seeds and cane syrup, formed into balls. They also make preserves and jelly from papaya, orange, cashew, and guava.

One of the classic island dishes is rundown. This is a stew consisting of fish, usually salted, especially salted cod fish, green plantains, cassava, potatoes, yams, breadfruit, dumplings, and sometimes cabbage, all cooked in coconut milk.

The percentage of literacy in San Andres and Providencia has always been the highest in Colombia. Even though many islanders still live off the land and from fishing, a large number pursue higher education. Dr. Jaime Gomez, in a book to be published soon, states that the islands have produced about 150 medical doctors during the last 100 years starting with doctor Zelotes Pusey.

The islands of San Andres and Providencia have produced many excellent navigators and sailors. These navigators are good at not only dead reckoning but also in celestial navigation. Dead reckoning is finding your position on the high seas without sophisticated instruments. Celestial navigation is using sun, moon, and stars. An example of this is Captain Richter, an American citizen of German descent, who had an unlimited master's license and had commanded many large steam ships but was not used to small ships. He left Miami in command of a banana boat with his crew of islanders. On passing the coast of Cuba his mates told him that his course would take him on the reef. He said, 'I am a captain with unlimited license and don't need to be told what to do by uneducated sailors.' He ran the ship onto the reef but, with some effort, was able to get free. On the way back with a load of bananas he tried to compensate by going too far from the Cuban coast and nearer to the Great Bahama Bank.

Captain Ulric Archbold, his second mate who was from Providencia, told him that he was going to miss Miami. Richter was not convinced of his position until they were in the latitude of West Palm Beach. This banana boat did not have any sophisticated navigational instruments on board. A sailor from Providencia did not need them but Captain Richter did. The captains of the sailing vessels from San Andres and Providencia were very efficient with the few navigational tools that they had. These tools were limited to a compass, a chart, a nautical almanac, a pair of dividers, parallel rulers, a sextant, and a chronometer (a clock). With these few instruments they traveled the seven seas.

Chapter 7—The Robinson Family

I have been asked several times, 'Where could a native of Colombia, one of the most Hispanic nations of all Latin America, get the name Robinson?' This question has been partially answered but here is the rest of the story.

Theodore Berelski

Let's start by saying that the story that Berelski was Henry Morgan's mate is false. Morgan lived in the seventeenth century and Berelski lived at the end of the eighteenth century into the first half of the nineteenth.

In the late eighteenth century, Russia overran Poland. In 1794 Prussia, Austria, and Russia decided to partition Poland. During the occupation several of the young men of Poland were forced to join the Russian army. Among these Polish youth was a young man by the name of Theodore Berelski. He was a strong Polish patriot and chafed under the Russian rule so he deserted the Russian army and joined the Polish underground under General Dabrowski.

In desperation these remnants of the Polish military, led by General Dabrowski, retreated to the West and tried to persuade Napoleon Bonaparte of France to chase the Russians out of Poland. He agreed to do so but persuaded them to help him in his war in Italy, France, and Austria.

In 1801 these Polish legions were reorganized into demibrigades and were sent to Haiti to try to put down the insurrection of the Haitians against France. The groups arrived in Haiti, one in May 1802, another on September 2, 1802, and a third on January 27, 1803. To make a long story short, the Haitians drove the Europeans into the sea.

Sixty of the Polish soldiers were assigned to the cutter Mosquito which had nine guns. The Polish then captured an American ship loaded with guns and ammunition. They then set the crew of the American ship adrift in a life boat and sold the ship to the Spaniards in Cuba.

The Polish pirates then captured several British ships and sold them to the Spaniards also. The British stationed in Jamaica dispatched the corvette warship Renard to pursue them. She was equipped with eighteen guns as opposed to the nine-gun Mosquito. The two ships met in the Bahama channel and the Mosquito, finding itself outgunned, started to run away, going around Cuba into the Gulf of Mexico, being followed in hot pursuit by the Renard. The Mosquito tried to escape capture by going into the harbor of Veracruz (now Mexico). The British ship waited at the entrance to the harbor. The Mosquito took advantage of a storm that came up and proceeded down the Central American coast with the Renard in hot pursuit.

The Mosquito, running out of food, anchored on the West side of Providencia and obtained food, water, and wood from the island. The Mosquito then left the island, minus one crew member, Theodore Berelski. The exact reason why Berelski stayed behind is not known but it is very possible that Berelski realized that the British would eventually capture them so he decided to abandon ship and settle there to make his home at Lazy Hill. The Mosquito was finally captured in the Gulf of Maracaibo with drastic results for the remainder of the crew.

Berelski was now a free man in Providencia. He was trying to escape the Russians, the French, the Americans, the British, and even possibly the Polish. Realizing that the people of Providencia were mostly English speaking and to avoid being captured he changed his name to John Robinson. It is noteworthy that in every generation since in the Robinson family there is both a Theodore and a John.

Berelski married an island girl by the name of Nancy Tayler. He also had a second wife, possibly common law, by the name of Mary Tayler, Nancy's sister. Berelski fathered nine children on the island of Providencia, eight boys and one girl. All the Robinsons from Colombia are descendants of John Robinson (Berelski). Berelski's daughter, Wilhemina Ann, married John C. Britton, the first Britton to come to the island, so all the Brittons are also descendants of Berelski.

Each one of these eight sons formed a clan of the Robinson family. I, Riva, come from the William clan, who is the youngest son of Nancy and Berelski. John Robinson had five sons by his wife, Nancy Tayler and three sons and one daughter by his second wife, Mary Tayler. Here are the eight Robinson clans: Julius and his children Eugenia, Archilas, Ana Arieta, Ellet, Ursula, Eudosia, Julius, Jr., and Amiel; John, Jr. and his children John III, Catherine, Mary Ann, Hermina, Louisa, and Adrian; Theodore and his children Sarah, Evinette, Arnat, Frederick, Theodore "Tim", Francis, and Sylvine; Alfred and his children Wiler, Percival, Feliciana, Elizabeth, Julius "Juke", Muriel, Alfred, Jr., Nancy, Euphemia, Teresa, Massa "Tick Soul," and Bunyan; and William and his children Ada, William, Jr., Angus, and Samuel. These children were with his first wife, Nancy. With his second wife, Mary, he had: Ambroise (whose children are unknown), Adrian (whose children are unknown), Adolfus and his son Philip; and Wilhemina Ann who married John Britton.

Nancy and Mary's father was William Tayler. He came from Liverpool, England and, according to historian J.C. Robinson, their mother was Mary Allen, a full blooded Miskito Indian.

Samuel Robinson was the son of William Robinson and grandson of Berelski and I am Samuel's grandson.

Tick-Sole's real name was Massa, but everybody knew him by "Tick-Sole." Tick-Sole was first cousin and close friend to Samuel Robinson, my grandfather. He often came to visit and often stayed overnight with him. Immediately behind the house of Samuel Robinson there's a rocky promontory. One day Tick-Sole came to visit, and being tired went to bed early while the rest of the family were up visiting. The bed where Tick Sole slept was a high, iron double bed. Pretty soon there was a loud thud. My grandmother, Eunice, shouted, "Tick-Sole, what happened?" To which he responded, "I was chasing a cow up the hill, and I stepped on a rock that slipped and I fell!"

The Kemble Family

The Kemble family originated in Germany. Early on some moved to Scotland so that today the Kembles trace their genealogy either to Germany or to Scotland. Stephen Kemble was an officer in the British navy at the time of the War of Independence of the colonies that became the United States of America. He had the title of colonel. He fought on the British side. After the war Colonel Kemble was sent by the British to Central America to take care of England's interests. In 1780 a ship under the command of Stephen Kemble took shelter from a hurricane in San Andres. In his diary Kemble wrote that he found 12 families on the island and that they cultivated very good cotton and raised some cattle.

Professor J.C. Robinson, head of the history department and dean of the University of California at San Bernardino, has done extensive research about Stephen Kemble and he states that Stephen Kemble had a son in Central America in what is now Nicaragua. This is denied in no uncertain terms by Peter Kemble, the patriarch of the very wealthy Kemble family of Manhattan, New York. Peter specifically denies that Stephen Kemble had any illegitimate children and added that Professor Robinson only wanted to get the Kemble money.

J. C. Robinson continues that Stephen Kemble's descendant, a son or grandson, settled in Providencia. His name was William Kemble.

Bill Kemble was the father of Leflet Kemble who is my mother, Crisilda's, father. Bill Kemble died when Leflet was 12 years old. Leflet's mother, Maclovia Buitrago, remarried. Leflet's stepfather ill treated him very much so he ran away from home, went to San Andres, and got a job with Abraham Rubenstein as a janitor. He worked himself up and became a partner with Rubenstein. After several years Leflet went into business for himself. He also became a prominent member of the Baptist church. He was an excellent musician and saw to it that Crisilda, his daughter, learned the organ and the mandolin. Leflet Kemble died prematurely of a superior aortic aneurism at the age of forty.

Charlie (Carlos) Robinson
This took place from the late 1800s to the present. My paternal grandfather, Samuel Robinson, worked for the Franklin Baker Co. as a buyer. This company produced coconut and chocolate products. Samuel Robinson did the buying for this company throughout Central America, but primarily in what is now Panama.

**Picture of Samuel Robinson and Eunice Blanford
and family
Front Row: Minnie, Samuel, Vida, Eunice, Vesto and
Annie
Back Row: Lizette, Ira, Walter and Crisilda**

Samuel was a young man at the time, and was engaged to marry Eunice Blanford

Knapp. For their honeymoon, Samuel, being a very thrifty man, took Eunice on his next buyer's trip. They went to the San Blas Islands to trade with the Kuna Indians.

So while Samuel was doing the business of buying with the men, Eunice, being half Indian herself, visited with the Kuna women.

During the day there was a small Indian boy who followed Eunice around everywhere she went. When evening came and the Robinsons were about to leave the island, this little boy was still hanging around. Eunice asked, "Where's this child's mother?" She was told that this boy was an orphan without mother or father. Eunice said, "If this boy has no parents, I'm going to be his mother." So she took this child to the ship on which they were traveling and on to her home in Old Providencia.

Eunice named the little boy, of about five or six years old, Charlie and treated him in every way as her own son. She sent him to school where he learned "The Three Rs." She also took him to church. Charlie was an extremely bright youngster, and readily absorbed both education and the Protestant religion. He grew up along and worked with my father and his siblings.

When Charlie reached adulthood he decided it was time for him to get married. But Charlie thought it only proper for him to marry someone of his own tribe. So he left Providencia and became a sailor, but then ended up in Nargana, capital of the San Blas Islands. Charlie was the only one of his tribe who knew "The Three Rs," so he became the Chief, not only of Nargana, but Chief of the entire Kuna nation.

Some traders would go to the San Blas Islands to buy coconuts. The buyer would ask the Indian, "How much does it cost for one thousand coconuts?" The Indian would say "$10.00." The buyer would say, "it is worth $5.00." The Indian would answer that, "no, it is $10.00." The buyer would then write on a piece of paper '$5.00' and show it to the Indian. The Indian would then say that if the paper says $5.00 then that must be right because the paper says so.

One of Charlie's main objectives was to stop the exploitation of his Indian people. Partially because of this his main thrust for the Indians was to get education to his people. He dedicated the rest of his life to this endeavor. Charlie also taught Protestant Christianity to the tribe, although at one time he had to cooperate with the Catholics in order to get his people educated.

The years passed and Samuel Robinson's grandson, Mario Robinson (my brother), became the president of the Panama Conference of Seventh day Adventists. Mario came to the U. S. for a General Conference Session in 1976. After the Session was over, Mario visited his parents, Walter and Crisilda Robinson, in Santa Maria, California. His father, Walter asked Mario if he had ever been to Nargana, San Blas Islands, and if he knew his uncle, Charlie Robinson. Mario answered, that Charlie Robinson had died the week before Mario had left Panama for the U. S. He said the story was in all the newspapers and that his coworkers at the Conference office, jokingly said to Mario that his relative Charlie Robinson had died. Mario said in addition, that he had been to Nargana, but was unsuccessful in bringing the Seventh day Adventist religion to the San Blas Islands.

At this point, Walter Robinson gave Mario the history of Charlie Robinson to which Mario responded that he would go to Nargana as soon as he got back to Panama.

So Mario went to Nargana when he returned to Panama, and made it a point to visit Charlie's sons. He introduced himself as their cousin. They protested that this was preposterous Mario is 6'2" and they are only 5'2." Mario's hair is curly and their hair is straight. So Mario gave Charlie's biography to them, as he had just recently learned from our father. Charlie's sons said, "Now just wait a minute!" and they produced Charlie Robinson's autobiography, which agreed 100% with what Mario had just told them. Needless to say, the religious meeting that Mario had that night was to a packed meeting house, and the Seventh day Adventist religion was established in the San Blas Islands. This shows God's leading over the past 100 years!

Now here is the rest of the story! In 2005, Mario, my other siblings and I went to the Island of San Andres, Colombia to a Family Reunion. When we were ready to return to the U. S., the airplane that was to pick us up to bring us to the U. S. crashed and killed all on board in Venezuela. Here also we see the Lord's hand in sparing our lives. So we had a 2-day delay. The flight we finally got to take us off the island routed us through Panama where we had a delay of approximately eight hours to board our plane to Los Angeles. During that time we were entertained in the airplane company's quarters reserved for VIPs. We were treated to all kinds of delicacies. We noticed the name tag on the person attending to us read 'Jarilo Robinson.' We told him that we were also Robinson, and both parties were overjoyed to find that Jarilo Robinson was Charlie Robinson's great grandson! We connected instantly and took many pictures with Jarilo. We have kept in contact ever since, and on our next trip of July and August of 2007, we had the privilege of going to Nargana and spending three wonderful days with Charlie Robinson's descendants.

My grandmother, Eunice Robinson, loved children and her three daughters inherited this same trait. Eunice had a maid from Southwest Bay, on the other side of the island of Providencia. One day the maid asked Eunice if she could take Annie, Eunice's youngest daughter, home with her for the weekend. Annie was five years old at the time. And so, Annie went with the maid. The maid's neighbor, who had eight children, just delivered twins. She told the maid she was not able to care for ten children. Annie spoke up, 'If you can't take care of them I will take this one.' The maid finally agreed to have the baby go with them just for a day or two. To make a long story short, Eunice took baby Minnie and raised her as if she were her own child. In fact, when grandfather Samuel died he included Minnie in his will and left her some of his property.

My father, Walter Robinson was a genius. When he was seven years old he was sent to school but he did not learn anything so he was taken out of school and kept at home. When he was eight years old his parents sent him to live with a lady in Bottom House and to study under a teacher named Watson from Jamaica. Walter then took off learning, so much so that he was put in charge of students who were much older than he. In eleven months he mastered from grades first through eighth.

After that he was put to study Shakespeare's works. Teacher Watson then made a trip to Nelly Downs to tell Samuel and Eunice, Walter's parents, to send Walter to England for further studies because he knew all that Watson could teach him. Samuel did not think this was necessary because he had his own ideas of education.

So from there on Walter taught himself accounting and celestial navigation. Starting at a very young age he would alternate between traveling the seven seas and coming home to work as an accountant.

On his first trip on an American ship he worked as a deck hand. The ship docked in New York. Groceries and supplies were brought on board for their voyage. Neither the purser nor the cook were on board at that time and no one else would check in the supplies. The deck hand Walter rose to the occasion and received the stores, taking account of every item. When the captain came on board he was so pleased with his deck hand, Walter Robinson, that he sent him to take the sailor's examination. He got the license of able bodied seaman, on the first try, which is the highest a non-U.S. citizen can go in the American Merchant Marines.

Walter Robinson and his two older brothers, Alva and Ira, were seamen. They traveled all over the world. Alva, the older of the three, never returned to Providencia. He called New Jersey home between trips. Sometimes the other two brothers worked on the same ship. Once they were both sailors on a Norwegian steam ship. Ira was a finicky eater. He would not eat eggs, chicken, pork, and only some types of fish but he liked pancakes. For several days he was enjoying pancakes for breakfast but he noticed that Walter was not eating any of the pancakes. 'Have some of these delicious pancakes, Walter,' Ira said. Walter said, 'Do you know what you're eating? That is not regular pancakes. That is pig's blood.' Ira almost threw up. He never ate pancakes again.

Ira and Walter looked somewhat alike, especially when they were young. Both of them had been traveling the seven seas for a few years when Walter went home for a vacation to Providencia. Walter greeted his mother Eunice warmly, then she said to him, 'Well, Ira, in all your travels have you seen Walter?' not realizing which of her sons had come home.

Jay Pong and the Mary V

Jay Pong was a Chinese gentleman who settled on the Island of Providencia. He worked hard and became relatively wealthy. He married the daughter of Frederick Robinson, who was the wealthiest man in Providencia at the time. Mr. Jay Pong was a merchant and had a large store. He also owned the Mary V, the most attractive and fastest sailing vessel of Providencia. Mary V was yawl-rigged, which is a two-masted sailing craft with the main mast in the bow, and the second mast was much shorter way aft (or to the stern). The Mary V traveled from Providencia to San Andres to Colon, Panama, and then would reverse its tracks. On one occasion, my father, Walter Robinson, who had been traveling the Seven Seas decided to come home, so he took a ship from New York to Panama, and found the Mary V docked in Colon and decided to ask for a passage to the Islands. He was greeted by Mr. Jay Pong, the owner, "Captain Robinson,

Captain Robinson! Boys, give Captain Robinson some suppah."

"I'm not hungry," Walter Robinson said, "I just want a passage to Providencia."

"Captain Robinson, you take my vessel to Providencia, because the captain was Captain Chung (Nicholas Newball), but Captain Chung doesn't do anything. He just says, "Ringalong, Ringalong, and stays in his bunk all day," and the boat gets to its destination. So I figure that Captain Luke and myself can say Ringalong, so I fired Captain Chung." Now Captain Chung was one of the most expert seamen from the Islands, and one of the most popular, and was especially good at dead reckoning.

Captain Luke was not a captain, but a very good sailor, but did not know the science of navigation. Mr. Jay Pong continued, "So Captain Luke and I brought the Mary V from Providence to San Andres to Colon, Panama. On the way back to San Andres, we traveled a week and could not find San Andres, so we turned and came back to Panama, reaching the San Blas Islands, and working our way up to Colon. Captain Robinson, I need you to take us home." So Walter took the Mary V to the Islands.

When my father told me this story, I asked, "Why couldn't they find the Islands?" He explained, "When going towards the continent you are bound to run into it somewhere, but it is quite difficult to find a speck of land out in the middle of the ocean! Also the trade winds are usually blowing from a southeasterly direction, and the sails are to the port (left) side of the vessel, and the current would have a northwesterly pull. But when Mr. Jay Pong was sailing, the wind was blowing from the Northwest, so the wind was pulling away from the Island, so he never found it. This was very fortunate because they could have run onto one of the reefs. I might add that I, Riva, made a recent trip to Providencia, and was told by Mr. Jay Pong's surviving son, Gimston, that he was so grateful that Walter Robinson had saved the Mary V and possibly his father's life.

Walter L. Robinson was the most eligible bachelor in all the Islands of San Andres and Providence. (In this story, I have changed some names so as not to offend.) There was a wealthy merchant in San Andres by the name of Juan Luna who had a daughter by the name of Lucinda. He was a millionaire according to reports of the people. Daddy started dating this girl and they finally got engaged. The custom then was that the suitor had to announce ahead of time that he planned to visit her, and then a chaperone was arranged for that date. He was a sea captain and came to San Andres and decided that since he was engaged to the girl, he wasn't going to announce his arrival. He went to see her unannounced and saw her in the garden smoking a cigarette. She never saw him. He said nothing, but turned around and never returned.

Other girls organized a picnic on Haines Cay. My mother, Crisilda, was invited to go since she was quite young and not considered a threat to anyone. Of course, the guest of honor was the intended eligible bachelor - Walter Robinson, the sea captain, was invited and he came.

They had a dance and each of the girls wanted to dance with Walter Robinson. But he wanted to dance with the youngster, Crisilda. So after dancing with the older girls, he asked Crisilda for a dance. It needs to be stated that Walter Robinson was a Seventh day Adventist and didn't know how to dance, since they don't believe in dancing. Crisilda had been taught well by her father how to dance. So Crisilda had to endure the 225 pound man on her toes every few steps. Walter told her right then that he'd like to get to know her better. She asked, "What about Lucinda?" Walter answered, "From now on everything with Lucinda is over." Here am I, Riva Robinson, the first son of the union of Walter and Crisilda—the only good thing I've seen to come from a cigarette!

From 1948 – 1950, I, Riva F. Robinson, was a seaman on the motor vessel, "Zesta." On a trip the ship stopped in Barranquilla, Colombia, where my Aunt Joyce lived, so I went to see her. Aunt Joyce asked me to go and visit some friends. This family had two beautiful daughters. The one daughter tried to start a friendship with me immediately. We had a very nice time together, yet I preferred the other sister. But I spent most of the time with the one who pursued me. When we were ready to leave, Aunt Joyce said, "What comes around goes around. The chip can't fall far from the block!"

"What do you mean by that, Tia?" I asked her.

Aunt Joyce said, "That lady is Lucinda Luna de Molina." Aunt Joyce then told me the preceding story about my father and mother and Lucinda. When I was talking with this girl, she said she wanted to marry a sea captain.

The first Seventh day Adventist baptism in Providence, included Eunice Robinson and her daughters, Estelle and Lizette, Lawrence Robinson, Charlotte Hawkins and her daughters, Julia and Muriel. Later my father was baptized when he was older.

The family of Samuel Robinson and the Family of Leflet Kemble, who married Henrietta Corpus, were all friends. The Kembles and the Corpuses were Baptists and the Robinsons were Seventh day Adventists. Eunice Robinson was a member of the first group to be baptized into the SDA Church in Providencia. Her husband, Samuel, although not baptized, was an active Seventh day Adventist. Samuel Robinson, the active soul winner that he was, had a subscription to "The Signs of the Times" sent to the Kembles, but they didn't know where it was coming from. The whole Kemble Family read the magazines when they came with interest, but didn't feel inclined to become Seventh day Adventists themselves. Samuel Robinson frequently visited his friends, the Kembles, and often took Walter along with him.

At this time, Crisilda and Walter were dating. Crisilda invited Walter to go with her to prayer meeting at the Baptist church one Wednesday night, where she was a member. Walter told her that he'd go if she'd go to services in his church also—agreed.

The sermon that was preached by Deacon Corpus of the Baptist Church that night was entitled, "Thou Art Weighed In The Balances And Found Wanting." Walter leaned over to Crisilda and whispered, "What are the balances?" At that very moment the deacon said, "The balances are the Ten Commandments!" My father, Walter, said to her, "Why aren't you keeping the Ten Commandments? So you must be found wanting!" Walter and Crisilda discussed the theme at length after the service was over. Walter discussed the topic extensively with Henrietta as well. Crisilda had unanswered questions in her mind after that.

The Leflet Kemble family all went one evening to the Baptist Church for prayer meeting. Aunt Adela, a young child at the time, fell asleep on the front bench. After the meeting the whole family went home. Finally, someone discovered that she was missing and returned to retrieve her.

Shortly after this, Leflet Kemble took ill and died with an aneurism of the superior aorta. Then after his death Henrietta became ill and died. During her illness Henrietta sent messages to Samuel Robinson three different times to come and see her because she had something to tell him. So, Samuel came to see her on three different occasions but each time she could not remember what she wanted to say. Finally, Samuel understood that she wanted him to care for her children until they reached adulthood. Before her death, Henrietta told Crisilda that she knew that Crisilda would eventually become a Seventh day Adventist, in spite of the fact that Leflet was a high officer in the Baptist Church and had encouraged his family to be faithful and true to their faith. Most people think that Henrietta died of a broken heart due to her husband Leflet's death.

Besides Samuel Robinson encouraging the Kembles toward the Adventist faith, Walter and Samuel were instrumental in having Crisilda take Adventist Bible studies from Rudolph Newball, who was in charge of the Adventist work on the Islands. Shortly after, Crisilda was baptized. Then she became more profoundly active in the church than my father!

When Walter and Crisilda became formally engaged they went to have their picture taken by Philip Philips, the main photographer of San Andres. Walter and Crisilda argued about how her hair should be, so it ended up to be the way neither one wanted it!

Photo of Walter and Crisilda Robinson

They were married by the judge, who after performing the ceremony said to Walter, "You may now kiss the bride."

Walter said, "We'll have plenty time for that!" And he didn't kiss her!

When I was a little boy there were no hotels on the islands. From time to time the missionaries of the Seventh day Adventist church would come to the islands to encourage the church members and to hold evangelistic meetings. Since there were no hotels the missionaries would have to stay in the homes of the church members who could accommodate them. Most of the time they would be at Walter Robinson's home. On one occasion Elder Norman Dunn and two other elders came to San Andres and, as usual, they stayed at the Robinson's home. Crisilda made cookies and pies for dinner. When she put those delicious pies to cool I, Riva, tried to taste the pie. 'Don't touch! That is for the people,' my mother said. When Elder Dunn came in for dinner three year old Riva said to him, 'Don't touch! This is for the people.'

My aunt, Alice Robinson, was married to Milton Downs. After she had five children, all boys, her marriage broke up and her family had to help her by taking some of her children in their homes. Walter and Crisilda took Roy, Aunt Alice's youngest son, into their home. One day Roy got a cigarette and started to smoke it. I, Riva, was about three years old. I ran into the house and shouted, 'Mama! Come quickly! Roy is steaming through his nose!' thinking that Roy had caught on fire and was burning up.

On another occasion Roy was staying with my grandparents in Providencia and we were living in San Andres. My father went to see his parents and took me along. We went on the schooner Peabody. We arrived at my grandparent's house at about 10 o'clock in the evening. My father knocked on the door and Eunice, my grandmother, said from the inside, 'Who is there?' 'It is I,' was the answer.

'I who?'

'I Walter.'

She said, 'Roy, get up and open the door.' Roy answered in patois, 'No de ya,' (there is no one there). The command was repeated several times and the same answer came back, no de ya, and as Walter kept knocking Eunice had to get up and let us in. On another occasion my grandfather told Roy to go to town and buy some rice, flour, and sugar. Roy asked if he could ride one of the horses. Grandfather answered no. Roy then said, 'May I ride a cow then?' 'If you are able, go ahead,' said grandfather. Believe it or not, Roy got a rope and rode the cow to town.

In our home there were eight children. We would fight among ourselves. To stop the fighting our mother gave all of us nicknames of flowers and told us that flowers don't fight. She even taught us a song about flowers. I was Myrtle, Arna was Dalia, Tulio was Red Rose and Mario, who was not yet four years old, was Lilly of the Valley. One morning Mario decided that he was going to school so, when no one was looking, he went down to the Catholic school about two blocks away. The nun who was the teacher, seeing a new pupil, said, "And what is your name little boy?" "Lilly o to bally" (Lilly of the Valley). She gave him some paper and some color crayons. At recess time the nun brought home a very happy little boy with his crayons. After that Mario was known as Lilly o to bally.

Sometime later, Spicer Jay Lung got married and the Robinsons were invited to the wedding. Our parents could not attend so the four older children were sent under my care. All went well until the middle of the reception when the cake was passed around. Mario was sitting next to me. It so happened that when the young lady serving the cake got to me it was the last piece of cake on the plate. I took it, of course, and Mario started to shout, "Give me piece, Riva! Riva, give me piece!" All the guests started to laugh.

When we were children our parents would take us to church. We were always sitting in the front pew. Then, between Sabbath School and the preaching service, we would be taken to Mrs. Elena May's home to go to the bathroom then brought back to church and not be permitted to go out, even to the toilet, during the church service. We liked to go to Mrs. Elena's because she would always give us cookies. This particular Sabbath we took the bus to church instead of a taxi. The road was very bumpy and full of pot holes. We got to the church and, as usual, sat in the front pew. Evidently, Mario had become car sick and suddenly he vomited all over himself and even the superintendent got messed up. Mario was taken to Mrs. Elena's house, given a bath, and came back to church dressed in pajamas that belonged to Mrs. Elena's niece, Gloria. At one time we lived in North End at Stanko on San Andres. At that time Stanko belonged to Arthur May. We also owned some chickens which we kept about one mile away. We also bought our milk from Mr. Maxi Velez so we would get up early, Tulio, Mario, and I, watched Mr. Velez milk the cows, got our milk, and on the way back fed the chickens and took the milk home in time for breakfast.

From time to time we were bothered by mosquitoes at night. One night when the moon was full the mosquitoes were exceptionally bad. We would be put to bed no later than 8:00 p.m. So we went to bed but the mosquitoes awakened us about 9 o'clock. We got up and asked our mother if it was time to go for the milk. She said, "No, go back to bed." The mosquitoes kept bothering, so in about half an hour we asked if it was time to get up. "No, go back to bed." After asking several times and with the mosquitoes bothering our parents so that they were sleeping poorly. Our mother not realizing what time it was said, "It is a little early, but you may go." So, Tulio, Mario, and I got up and went for the milk. We got to Mr. Velez's house but he was not milking the cows. We waited a little but no one stirred so we got the idea that we would go and feed the chickens. We went and called the chickens and reluctantly they came down from their roost. They ate and went back to their rest. We then returned to Mr. Velez's property and everything was quiet so we went next door and lay down under Mr. Manuel's ginep tree and went to sleep on the ground until morning.

Usually, wherever our mother went she took her children with her. One afternoon she was going on an errand and took her six children that she had at that time: Riva, Arna, Tulio, Mario, Zita, and Loida (Lisa and Efren came later). They passed the house of the Davis's where Mrs. Davis was standing by the gate. "Good evening Mrs. Davis," my mother greeted her. "Me sweet. What a lot of pickniny," exclaimed Mrs. Davis. My mother responded, "How many children do you have?" Ten was the answer. "I only have six. Count them," answered my mother.

As stated above we lived in Stanko in an apartment on the second floor. The back side of Stanko was in the sea on stilts so our back porch was over the water. One morning my sister, Zita, was on the porch looking out at the sea below. Suddenly she called me, "Come look! What do you think that is floating on the water," she asked. "That is money," I answered. I rushed downstairs and found several American bills as well as some Colombian money. I told Zita, "We are rich!" About half an hour later a fisherman, Mr. Manuel, came by and asked if by any chance we had seen some money. "Yes, I have it but you need to pay me a fee for returning it," I said. Mr. Manuel lived in a hut and did not dare leave his life savings in the hut so he put all his money in his pocket and went to work on his fishing boat. He leaned over from the wharf and the money fell out into the sea without him noticing. Anyway, he was glad to give Zita and me a few dollars for finding his money. When our father came home from work that evening we told him of our good fortune. "What! You took some of that poor man's life savings?! You go and give him back every cent. That money is not yours." So much for being rich.

When Zita was eight years old we were living in Providencia at our grandparent's home. Our Aunt Joyce, our mother's sister, lived in Colon, Panama. Aunt Joyce asked our mother to let Zita come to Colon for a short visit so she went on the Yawl Mary V. Zita was just learning to read. Some of the sailors got into an argument as to where is the Lord's Prayer found in the Bible. None of them could find it. Finally, a sailor said, "This little girl is from a religious family. She should know where to find the Lord's Prayer." He handed her the Bible and believe it or not she turned to it to the amazement of the sailors. Zita remained several weeks in Panama then returned home.

All the water for drinking and household use in Providencia at that time was obtained from the rain. The houses had gutters on the roofs that drained the water into a tank or cistern. Our grandparent's front porch was the top of their cistern. The cistern was completely covered excepting for the opening where the gutters entered and for a trap door where water was drawn using a bucket. Zita was sent to draw some water. She let down the bucket into the cistern after opening the trap door. When Zita tried to pull out the bucket she fell into the cistern and the trap door slammed shut behind her. The water was deep, needless to say. Mario was playing nearby. He was one year older than Zita. Mario opened the trap door just as his sister came to the surface. He grabbed her arm and held her until our mother, Crisilda, came and pulled her out of the cistern. It was Mario who saved his sister's life.

When we were children living in Providencia at our grandparent's home for the first time a road was being built around the island. The builders found the type of gravel that was needed in Samuel Robinson's back yard so they dug out the gravel, leaving a large hole. The rains came and filled the hole with water. One day our grandmother, Eunice, was in the greje, the secondary kitchen. Loida at the time was about two years old and was playing in the yard. Grandmother looked out the window and she saw two little legs go under the water. She yelled, "Cris! Cris! Sam! Sam! The baby is in the water!" Our mother, Crisilda, ran, jumped into the hole full of

91

water, even though she could not swim, and saved baby Loida from drowning, an example of a mother's love.

The Mary V on a Stormy Voyage

Crisilda inherited a large 3-story house from her parents. She, Walter and the family lived there after they were married. After several years, Walter wanted his own house, so they sold the big house in San Andres at a cheap price, and decided to build a house in Providencia. This was not just to be any house. All the houses on the Islands were of wood or thatched material. He decided to build his house of bricks—the very first house on the Islands of cement. So he figured how many bricks he needed, and bought them in Cartagena. These were more bricks than one small Island vessel could carry, so he sent part of the bricks on the Mary V to Providencia and the rest on a schooner by the name of the Rembrandt. Walter sent his wife and children on the Mary V while he followed on the Rembrandt.

It was a beautiful afternoon when the Mary V left Cartagena and we cleared Boca Chica, taking in a gorgeous sunset. But soon the winds began to blow, and we who were enjoying the moonlit evening on deck had to scramble for shelter. My (Riva's) pillow was blown overboard. The wind got fierce and increased to storm force. All the sails had to be taken in with the exception of the standing jib and a double-reefed jigger sail (mizzen). There was a large steam ship going in the same direction, but we were going faster with the small amount of sail that we had! For the next 5 days, neither sun nor stars were visible, and no one knew what our precise position was. When the sun finally came out, we took a sight, and we found ourselves almost to Jamaica! So we had to turn and arrive at Providencia via Roncador Cay. The people in Providencia had given up the Mary V as lost along with us, but were happily surprised to see us even though it was from the Northeast instead of the expected southeast. What a price for bricks and a new house!

When they were unloading the Rembrandt, they loaded a canoe with bricks, then put Tulio, my younger brother, in the loaded canoe to take him to shore, but the canoe with the bricks started to sink, so one of the men in the canoe took Tulio, and threw him in the air. He was caught by someone on deck of the larger vessel. The canoe sank with the bricks, and they had to be retrieved by divers.

Walter's Folly

Walter tried to build this house by himself. He dug the foundation down 6' until he found solid rock. But he didn't realize he needed a plumb line, & the bricks started to fall down, so he got expert masons from Cartagena to build his house. Because Providencia was exposed to frequent hurricanes, the house had to be built strong enough to withstand them. The foundation was built 6' deep and steel bars were placed at the four corners of the house, going from the foundation up to the roof. There were gutters to catch the rain water to be drained into a 10,000 gallon cistern. Needless to say, this was a unique, but strong house by the time it was finished. There were 3 bedrooms, a living room, dining room, kitchen and bathroom. The only part of the house that the roof was not bolted down was the bathroom roof.

The people of Providencia, having never seen a brick house before, but only houses made of wood or thatched material, were very amused, and gave the house the name of "Walter's Folly." The people said the house with the next hurricane winds would fall.

When the next hurricane came on October 20, 1940, two of the most critical people were two fishermen who were brothers. Two days before the hurricane, I was sent to buy fish from these same men. These fishermen were very accurate with the weather. They knew two days before the hurricane by the large oceans swells that a hurricane was approaching, so one of the fishermen whose name was Dillion, was making a big joke to his customers by saying, "A hurricane is coming, and we'll see what happens to 'Walter's Folly'." So two days later the wind started to pick up. The barometer was falling fast. Walter came home early from work, and tied down all the gutters on the house. He fastened everything he could, and we all anxiously waited for the storm to hit. At 10 p.m. the wind was blowing from the northeast at 120 mph, accompanied by torrential rain. Pretty soon there was a knock on the door, and the neighbor lady with her children asked for shelter because her house had blown away. In about half an hour another family knocked on the door, seeking shelter. At about 1 a.m. the wind seemed to have stopped. I said, "Daddy, it's over."

He answered, "No, me son—the worst is yet to come!" He was saying indirectly that we were only in the eye. But alas, in about 20 minutes, the wind returned from the southeast this time with increased fury. Then the bathroom roof which had not been bolted down blew away, but the remainder of the house didn't even shake.

There was another knock on the door, and this time it was the fisherman who had so loudly ridiculed "Walter's Folly" a few days before, and he was asking for shelter!

This reminds me of the children's song about the story in Matthew 7 of the Bible:

"The wise man built his house upon the rock—and it stood firm!"

By morning, the storm had started to abate. More than ¾ of the houses on the Island were destroyed. The next day, Tulio and I were sent to Lazy Hill to make sure our cows were still alive. On the way we had to pass Old Town, of course, and we paused to see if the most beautiful house in Old Town was still there. Our house was built on a high promontory just above the beach, but founded on rock. Before the house was built, I, Riva, said to my father, Walter, "Dad, please build the house right on the beach where it's so beautiful." But he paid no attention to my advice, and dug his foundation 6' down until he found solid rock, and "It stood firm."

Anyway, this house in Old Town was right on the beach, and it was the most beautiful sight to behold. But after the hurricane no part of it was to be found, and no one has ever seen any part of it since—it must have blown out to sea. "The foolish man built his house on the sand, and the house on the sand went splash!" (end of the song)

When the hurricane hit, my mother was seven-months pregnant with my youngest brother, Efren. She made "Johnny Cake" (a type of biscuit made with coconut milk) and mint tea for those seeking shelter in the house.

On another occasion we were in Cartagena in a rented house which was on the road to the city's cemetery. Whenever someone died the funeral procession had to pass our house. One day there was a dead lady being taken to be buried. The coffin was borne by six men. The priest led the funeral party. Just after the procession went by our house the lady in the coffin started to kick. The men carrying the coffin dropped it and started to run away. Even the priest was confused. Most of the people in the procession ran also. There was, however, one man who had sufficient presence of mind to open the coffin and the lady in the coffin started to scream. I am told that this lady lived several more years. It must be explained that the custom was to bury the dead within twenty-four hours of passing away. No one was embalmed or frozen in those days.

One morning when we lived in Stanko in San Andres I was standing on the front porch with my father when a big strong man who was a sailor and whose name was Tibbits passed by. I could not help but admire his healthy looking physique and his big muscles. He went into the bar across the street. That evening when my father came home I heard him calling me from the front porch. What I saw was Tibbits staggering down the street and two boys throwing stones at him. Tibbits tried to defend himself by picking up dirt and throwing it at the boys. The boys just laughed and continued to hit him with stones. My father said to me, "Riva, my son, that is what drink does to a man." I have never needed another temperance lecture.

When my father had the business of processing coconuts into copra, the man who sold him the coconuts came to have a business conference with my father and during that time this man, Jeremiah Lynton, stayed at our house. In our home my mother always made sure that we had morning and evening worship. This particular morning Mr. Lynton was asked to offer the morning prayer. He evidently thought that Walter's children had too good an appetite because in his prayer he said, 'And God, help these children not to eat their parents into the poor house.'

Going to Medellin

As children we were home schooled. To be sure we were not deprived socially, in three of those years my parents accepted other students so that we had a private school in our home where the teachers were Crisilda and Walter Robinson, so that up to the eighth grade my only teachers were my parents. At that point, my parents decided that their children should have additional education. It was economically impossible to send the children away to school so they sold everything they owned in the islands, their house, their land, everything, and moved to the continent. Walter started the coconut processing business but went bankrupt when the American destroyer collided with the Envoy.

My parents did not let this disaster keep them from educating their children. Crisilda and the children traveled to the city of Medellin and rented a house near the Instituto Colombo Venezolano so that we all could get a higher education while living at home. No one had to live in the dormitory and pay extra fees.

Family of Walter and Crisilda Robinson; Front Row: Loida, Efren, Crisilda, Arna and Lisa; Back row: Riva, Tulio, Mario and Zita

In the meantime, my father signed on to the U.S. Merchant Marine to take supplies to the war zone in Europe. When Germany was defeated, he moved to the Pacific war zone. We, his family, did not see him for four years until he came home on a short vacation. When he arrived he embraced his children one by one. Then he asked, 'Where is Lisa?' Our mother answered, 'She is right beside you.' Our father hugged her and exclaimed, 'I thought she was one of the neighbor's children!' He did not recognize his own daughter.

My sister Arna had always wanted to be a nurse. While she was still a student in high school in Medellin, Colombia, she read everything she could find about nursing, especially about maternity and delivering babies. Even though she had not had any formal training she thought that she had acquired sufficient knowledge from her reading, that in a pinch she could deliver a baby. Lola was a single mother who lived next door to us in Medellin. She was about to have a baby and could not afford a doctor. Arna offered her prenatal counseling and told her that when she was in labor to call her. Very early one morning while it was still dark, Lola sent someone to get Arna. Quickly she grabbed a pair of scissors and some thread, then she started out the door. At that moment, Crisilda Arna's mother, called to her, "Where are you going? Don't you leave this house." This was one of the few times in her life that Arna disobeyed her mother. She ran out the door and over to where Lola was living. She found Lola in severe pain. Suddenly, the baby came with a big rush for which Arna was not prepared and it frightened her. She remembered however, to tie and cut the umbilical cord. She then cleaned up the baby, and then had another scare when Lola delivered the placenta. She helped Lola get cleaned up. Both Lola and her baby daughter survived the ordeal in great shape. Arna remembers her first delivery with a certain amount of satisfaction.

To make a long story shorter, all eight children are now professionals. We all have a tremendous debt of gratitude to our parents for their sacrifice, for a mother, being without her husband for so many years and raising a bunch of rambunctious teenagers by herself and our father, risking his life by going to work in the war zone in World War II.

All of my brothers and sisters and myself, after finishing our schooling in Medellin, Colombia, and working for a time, one by one we came to the United States for further education. Then we all settled in the U.S.A. and all became U.S. citizens so we all have dual citizenship. Even though we live in the U.S. any time an opportunity presents itself we return for a vacation to our island home.

When Tulio first came to the United States he took a plane from Chicago to Los Angeles International Airport. After deplaning he hailed a taxi and told the driver to take him to Loma Linda thinking that Loma Linda was in the Los Angeles area. The taxi driver took Tulio, his wife Esther, and their baby Mildred (Mimi) to Loma Linda, sixty-five miles away where they arrived just in time for our sister, Arna's, wedding reception. Needless to say that the taxi fare took all the money that Tulio had. Their second child, Adela, was born the very next day in Loma Linda.

On another occasion Tulio and Esther went to Colombia for a vacation. They decided to go from Bogota to the coast by train in order to see the country. The train stopped for a few minutes in a little town, then started again slowly, picking up speed. Just then a man picked up Tulio's satchel,

containing all their money, their credit cards, and even their
U.S. passports. Esther grabbed the man by the shirt but had to
let go to avoid being stabbed. The man then jumped from the
moving train. They arrived in Santa Marta minus their money,
their passports, and their credit cards. Fortunately, they went
to the best hotel in Santa Marta and the hotel made a call to
the U.S. and they got in touch with Mimi who gave the hotel
their credit card numbers. They then got to Barranquilla and
went to the company where Tulio had worked for 5 years
several years before. No one there recognized the former
treasurer of the company and would not lend him any money.
One of the employees said that they knew some Robinsons in
the city. These Robinsons turned out to be Tulio's first
cousins, Leopold and Alva, who came and took them to their
home. They still were without their passport or any other
identification. Finally they went to the American consulate
and told the consul their problem. The consul questioned
them extensively and was finally convinced that they were
true U.S. citizens and gave them temporary passports so that
they were able to get back home.

My Siblings

Photo of Walter and Crisilda Robinson and Family
Back Row: Arna, Mario, Zita, Tulio, Lisa, Efren,
Loida and Riva
Front Row: Walter and Crisilda

A few words about each of my siblings: Arna is a nurse
and gives lectures and classes. She is married to Dr. Gordon

Gilkes a medical doctor. They have two children, Lucia, who is a nurse, and Gordon, Jr.

Tulio became an accountant and was a treasurer of the Seventh day Adventist conferences in Colombia, Costa Rica, and Guatemala and an accountant in the Pacific Union Conference of Seventh day Adventists in Thousand Oaks, California. His wife is Esther Gonzalez and they have three children, Mildred, who is a nurse, Adela, who is a nurse practitioner specializing in cardiology, and Tulio, Jr., who is an anesthetist.

Mario is an ordained minister of the Seventh day Adventist church and has been president of the Colombian Island Mission, acting president of Costa Rican Mission, president of the Panama Conference of Seventh day Adventists, and pastor of several churches. Mario is a concert pianist and has given concerts in Europe, South America, Central America, the Caribbean, and the United States. He is married to Elsa Heronimus and they have four children, Magda, who is a medical doctor, Rose Marie, a mathematician, Glenda, who is a teacher and school administrator, and Mario, Jr., who is an aviation mechanic.

My sister Zita is a teacher and school administrator in Colombia, Costa Rica, and the United States.

My sister Loida is a city administrator and manager of several medical and dental offices. She is married to Orvil Archbold who is a sea captain and an accountant. They have four children, Janice, who is an attorney, Karen, who is an accountant, Neil, who has had several positions with different companies, and Nubia a nurse, who is now deceased.

My sister Lisa has a masters degree in medical technology and worked for the White Memorial Medical Center as a bacteriologist and she has worked as a bacteriologist for the state of California.

Efren is a medical doctor. He had his own medical practice and has worked for the state of California also. He is married to Elvira Alvidrez and they have three children, Lizette, who is a physical therapist, Efren, Jr., who owns his own furniture business, and Sonia, who is a registered nurse.

I, Riva Fidel Robinson, have had several professions: accountant, navigator, college professor, medical doctor. I am now an old man and retired. I am married to Vivien Townsend. She is a famous pianist and singer. We have four children.

Photo of Riva and Vivien Robinson and family
Back row: Richard, Riva, Vivien and Ron
Front Row: Rhonda and Riva, Jr.

My son, Riva, Jr., is an ordained minister of the Seventh day Adventist church. He is pastor of three churches at the present time, two in English and one in Spanish. Riva is married to Luz Marina Angulo and they have three children, Erika, Ryan, and Andrew.

My second son is Ronald, who is a psychologist and works for Berrien County in charge of mental health in Niles, Michigan. He lives with his partner, Joseph Gress, and has two children, Abbe and Peter.

My daughter is Rhonda, who is a medical doctor. She is married to Roland (Bert) Ringer who is a recruiting officer for Southern Adventist University in Tennessee. She has two stepsons, Clayton and Austin, and two adopted daughters, Summer and Anastasia.

My youngest son is Richard, who is an accountant of the state of California. He lives with his partner, Tim Burkhart, in Vacaville, California.

Now a few anecdotes of my immediate family: When Riva, Jr. was a little boy he asked where the various animals came from. Among his questions was, 'Where do the chickens come from?' I told him that the hen lays the eggs, then sits on them for several days, then the chickens are hatched. That night, without being noticed, Riva, Jr. went to the refrigerator, took twelve eggs out of a carton, put them in his bed, and slept on them. The next morning Riva, Jr. had broken eggs all over him.

Once every year our church members have the custom of inviting our neighbors to help us with offerings, especially for medical work. Even the children are given little cans and they go to the neighbors who drop coins into their cans, then the children turn the cans into their church. One year, after this ingathering, as it was called, was over, my son Ronald got himself a second can and solicited offerings but used the money to buy himself candy. He did not let his parents know what he had done, knowing that he would be punished. He revealed this secret to me after he was a grown man.

Another time I took our car to the mechanic. Ron went along. When we got to the mechanic's shop I noticed a pop bottle on the ground and I told Ron, 'Don't touch that bottle,' then I went to talk with the mechanic. I soon glanced over at Ron. He took the bottle to his mouth and took a big gulp, then started to cough violently, then to cry. He did not like the taste of gasoline.

I took my medical internship in Saskatoon, Canada. For the most part we enjoyed it, in spite of the very cold winter. The temperature went down to fifty-two degrees below zero without the wind chill. For two weeks the temperature did not get any higher than thirty below. One winter day we told Rhonda to take the pail outside and empty it. After a few minutes Rhonda did not return and so I went outside to investigate. There was Rhonda, seated in the pail, stuck to the ice. She had slipped on the ice and fallen into the pail in a sitting position. The pail stuck to the ice and the water in the pail froze around Rhonda and she could not get up. She almost froze to death. It does get cold in Saskatoon. When one goes to town in Saskatoon the car has to be plugged into a heater or one would never be able to start it up.

When I was in medical school in Guadalajara, Mexico, one day the children asked if they could go riding their bicycles. I put the bicycles in our van and took them out to the Barrancas (a cliff at the edge of town). They were going to ride down to the river below. I told them to ride carefully, not to drink any water out of the river and I would pick them up. About a week later we went to the beach for a long weekend. While there Ron became very irritable and by the time we returned home he was running a high fever. I took him to a specialist who was a professor at the university and the diagnosis came back as typhoid fever. We started treatment but he became delirious. He had drunk some water from that river. There was a lull in the fever for a few hours, and then he got worse. Now he had also an acute abdomen. An internist saw him and told us to get a surgeon right away. We hospitalized Ron and got the best surgeon in Guadalajara, Professor Dr. Agustin Rios. Dr. Rios came in looking very confident and sure of himself. He examined Ron and his countenance fell. He said, "He needs emergency surgery and only has a fifty-fifty chance of surviving." Ron was then taken to surgery immediately and I was permitted to watch. In the meantime I called to my relatives in the United States to offer special prayer for Ron's life. Dr. Rios, on opening Ron's abdomen, found his gallbladder to be the size of a large avocado, black and gangrenous. The gallbladder was removed and Ron was sent to recovery in very serious condition. The next morning he was conscious. When the nurse, who was a nun, came in that morning she said to him, "You almost went to heaven last night." His answer was, "Oh, no I did not." Ron recovered and today he is 6'2" and weighs 265 lbs.

We took our dog, Suzy, to Mexico with us when I was in medical school. The house in which we lived had ceramic tile floors. One day my youngest son, Richard, who was quite young then, was coming down the stairs. The stairs had no railing and he fell off the stairs from about eight feet high onto the concrete tile floor, hurting himself. Our pastor was visiting at that moment and our dog, Suzy, thinking that he was the cause of Rick's fall, almost tore the pastor to pieces.

Just before my retirement I was working for the state of California in the prison system. The head of the department of dentistry, Dr. Bonett, asked me one day, "Riva, why did you leave Colombia and come to the United States, anyway?" I answered, "Well, it is like this: when I was young I lived in a nice house at the beach. I owned a sail boat and I owned horses. I got rid of the house at the beach, I got rid of the sail boat, and I sold the horses. I came to the United States to get an education so that I could make a lot of money, buy a house on the beach, get a sailing yacht, and buy horses." I am still waiting to accomplish this.

Bibliography

Archbold, Britton Marco. *Principios de los Relatos Historicos y Anecdotas Sobre el Archipelago de San Andres y Providencia y Sus Habitantes,* Buletin de la Sociedad Geografica de Colombia, vol. 20.

Cabrera, Ortiz Wenceslao. *San Andres y Providencia Historia,* Editorial Cosmos, Bogota, Colombia, 1980.

Chow, Lina. *Adonde ha Ido lo que no Volvera,* Cali, 2008.

Duffis, Daniel A. *A Blessed Heritage: the History of the Seventh Day Adventist church in San Andres and old Providence Islands.*

Edwards, Jay. *Social Linguistics: San Andres and Providencia Islands, Colombia,* University of Michigan, Ann Arbor.

The Kuna Indians of Panama

Kupperman, Karen. *Providence Island: 1630 – 1641,* Cambridge University Press, 1993.

Parsons, James. *San Andres and Providencia,* Beverly Hills University of California Press, 1956.

Petersen, Walwin. *The Province of Providence,* The Christian University of San Andres, Providence, and Catalina, San Andres Island, Colombia.

Robinson, J. Cordell. *Genealogical History of Providencia Island,* California State University, San Bernardino, Borgio Press.

Tornage, Loren. *Island Heritage,* Cali, Colombia, 1975.

Wilson, Peter. *Crab Antics,* New Haven Yale University Press, 1973.

Wilson, Peter. *Oscar: an Inquiry into the Nature of Sanity,* Random House, 1974.